DATE DUE		

THE INTELLECTUAL REVOLUTION IN TWELFTH-CENTURY EUROPE

THE INTELLECTUAL REVOLUTION IN TWELFTH-CENTURY EUROPE

Tina Stiefel

ST. MARTIN'S PRESS
New York

© 1985 Tina Stiefel
All rights reserved. For information, write:
St. Martin's Press, Inc., 175 Fifth Avenue, New York, NY 10010
Printed in Great Britain

First published in the United States of America in 1985

Library of Congress Cataloging in Publication Data

Stiefel, Tina
    The intellectual revolution in twelfth century
    Europe.
    Bibliography: p.
    Includes index.
    1. Civilization, Medieval—12th century. I. Title.
    CB354.6.S75   1985   509′.021   85-18275

ISBN 0-312-41892-2

Contents

For Tamara and Samuel

Preface

When I conceived the idea for this book, I believed that the times required a fresh evaluation of the origins of European scientific thinking. The advances in the sociological, economic and anthropological studies of the medieval period strongly suggested that a new look at the intellectual history of the twelfth century was in order. My book is a small contribution to the extensive work of Charles Homer Haskins, Gordon Leff, E.J. Dijksterhuis, Sir Richard Southern and A.C. Crombie – scholars who have approached the middle ages free from the pressure of conservative historical tradition.

I am grateful for the encouragement given me by the late Marshall Baldwin, Sir Richard Southern, Gordon Leff and A.C. Crombie, and I am indebted as well to Peter Dronke for his seminal work in medieval studies, and to Peter Brown for the acuity of his historical perceptions. Heartfelt thanks to Professor Jill Claster for her unfailing encouragement, and to Professor Joseph Salemi for his unstinting assistance and moral support. I deeply appreciate the support of family and friends during much disheartening travail.

Happy is he who partakes of knowledge of science . . . contemplating the ageless order of deathless Nature – how it came to be formed, its manner, its way.

(Euripides)

Introduction

In the early part of the twelfth century the world was seen for the first time since antiquity as wholly and legitimately open to human inquiry. How did this perspective originate and what forms did it take? This book proposes a revision in the thinking about an important topic in the history of thought, a topic that has been largely ignored. It is an interpretative essay on an undercurrent of sceptical rationality, which surfaces but rarely in western history. Although historians have observed aspects of this development, a full exploration of its implications has not yet been presented.

The study places this event in the context of a complex social development. Towns in the eleventh century grew increasingly prosperous while remaining part of an essentially agricultural society. The emerging urban culture, enriched by increasing travel and the consequent cross-fertilisation of ideas, produced a dramatic shift in attitude among the more adventurous minds of the time. A free secular mentality was superimposed upon a traditional one imbued with the magical thinking of an oral culture. The prerequisites of an open and questioning intellectual ambience necessarily are a substantial degree of political stability and freedom from the more debilitating constraints of physical want.

The resulting release of mental energy produced a deep thirst for new ideas. A remarkable intellectual ferment was engendered among men sensitive to these conditions, and such bold thinkers as Adelard of Bath, William of Conches and Thierry of Chartres, among others, found themselves entranced by the spirit of reason. Their purpose was to approach all experience objectively, consciously allowing for doubt, paradox and uncertainty. The new rationalist impulse turned some toward Roman law and its implications for systematic and categorical thought; others used satirical poetry as a means of critical analysis of society; and stonemasons, in creating a new species of cathedral, were propelled to invent highly original engineering devices.

The most daring of all intellectual enterprises at this time, however, was the concern central to the thinking of the men named above and their disciples: the strict application of critical, analytical thinking to all aspects of natural phenomena. Relying upon their faith in natural causation and in the atomist structure of the basic substance of the cosmos, they postulated and imaginatively attempted to formulate a rational methodology for the investigation of *rerum natura*; they invented for themselves a new discipline — natural science.

For the purposes of this book, the term 'rationalism' is defined as a pragmatic, unorthodox and nonconformist cast of mind, rather than an exercise in abstraction. It embraces sceptical, empirical, uncertain, provisional and potentially unsettling forays into every kind of human experience as well as into organised thought. The movement described in this study was initiated by men who called themselves *moderni*, who were attempting to find new paths — to break out of the mould of traditional thought. The term cosmologist has been applied to the writers here considered; perhaps it would be more accurate to describe them as proto-scientists. The Greeks had taken the same step 17 centuries earlier and it would be another 6 centuries before the mood reappeared during the Enlightenment. The rationalist movement I discuss here represents the only appearance of this rare phenomenon between the ancient world and the modern one. It should be emphasised, however, that 'rationalist' is used in the loose sense described above, with a wide connotation including the qualities of open inquiry, creative hypothesising and the impulse to apply it to a broad spectrum of human experience which included science, medicine, law, government, literature and architecture.

My thesis can be summarised briefly. The prevailing estimate of medieval thinking about science is inaccurate on several counts. In my view, productive ideas concerning nature as a fit subject of objective inquiry were articulated in Western Europe before the appearance of the Aristotelian corpus in translation. These ideas and approaches to the natural sciences which were expressed then were influenced in part by Arab scientific thought, scattered bits of Greek science and medicine, and the Chalcidius' version of Plato's *Timaeus*. A new approach to the systematic study of science was formulated by these men a century before the work on this subject was done by Grosseteste and Roger Bacon. This approach was an adumbration of a scientific methodology, which included the inductive, empirical, mathematical and deductive techniques, although there was no organised presentation *per se* made of it. It is the random and scattered nature of the material on science that accounts, I believe, for the fact that its full significance has hitherto been missed. The twelfth-century thinkers were quite aware of the inferences to be drawn from their work; they promoted their ideas with great courage and energy in the hope of stimulating an intellectual revolution. Although their works were widely read during the following three centuries, they failed to bring about the revolution they sought, for the times were unpropitious for such a radical change.

This study is organised around a number of unconnected passages culled from several twelfth-century treatises, illustrating the following points:

1. That a rational and objective investigation of nature in order to understand its operations is possible and desirable.

2. That such an investigation might make use of techniques of mathematics and deductive reasoning.

3. That it should use empirical methodology — i.e. evidence based on sense-data, where possible.

4. That the seeker for knowledge of nature's operations (a 'scientist') should proceed methodically and with circumspection.

5. That the scientist should eschew all voices of authority, tradition and popular opinion in questions of how nature functions, except to the extent that the information is rationally verifiable.

6. That a scientist must practise systematic doubt and sometimes endure a state of prolonged uncertainty in his disciplined search for an understanding of natural phenomena.

The organising principle of my work is to show that these six points constitute a fairly articulate and explicit programme, and that they are evidence of a clear and distinct appreciation of science as a category of human endeavour worthy of serious interest. In sum, this is a study of the inception of a belief in a rationally ordered universe and the concomitant search for a discipline of natural science in medieval Europe.

This study departs from the traditional historical approach in that it offers new suggestions, alternatives and perspectives on an aspect of medieval thought. As A.C. Crombie has perceptively said, 'Historiography is a dialogue between an interrogating present and an interrogated past. Separated forever from that living past, interrogating historians in following their proper art can reconstruct only from what they see and understand.'[1] My approach is along similar lines: I see my task as that of investigating a distinct mentality relating to the concept of science.

Medievalists tend to see their subject in a special light, one which floods their period with nostalgic beauty. The march of a glorious ascent to a rich 'synthesis' of classical and Christian traditions, reaching its summit in the works of Aquinas and Dante, is a deeply cherished vision to be taught and defended. The emotional allegiance to this view, strengthened in our time by the afterglow of the Romantic and Pre-Raphaelite fantasy, is difficult to shake.

But shaken it must be: our knowledge now of this thousand-year span makes such views absurdly anachronistic, and far too simple. My view is that the middle ages is a term of very limited value. For example, the period in Western Europe between 1080 and 1150 was a time of great diversity of social, economic and intellectual experience, markedly different from those of the succeeding 50 years. (Is it not time to dispense with the category of centuries as useful historical units?) In this book I firmly reject all of these hallowed historical traditions, although I know that in so doing I will inevitably antagonise some scholars. My aim is to widen the reader's understanding of an historical development for the purpose of further exploration of a field which deserves more scrutiny than it has yet received.

The book offers a fresh interpretation of the writings of these twelfth-century cosmologists. Building on the pioneering work of Charles Homer Haskins and the seminal studies in medieval science of A.C. Crombie, this book is a study of the social and intellectual consequences of the eleventh-century urban development in Western Europe. An optimistic mood evolved which permitted a trust in the efficacy of the trained intellect and its application in the real world for practical purposes. A belief in human progress was implicit in the thought of the cosmologists, and a connection between scientific advancement and social reform was clearly articulated. Till now we have had two enlightenments to ponder — that of the ancient Greeks and that of the eighteenth century. The evanescent but brilliant flash of intellectual light that made an appearance in the twelfth century is not unworthy of some scrutiny and, in view of the historical circumstances surrounding it, considerable wonder.

Note

1.   A.C. Crombie, 'What is the History of Science?' *The Times Higher Education Supplement* (London, 3 February 1984), p. 15.

1 The Intellectual Background

'Intellect is the swiftest of things, for it runs through everything.' (Thales of Miletus)

In order to present the conceptual revolution of the twelfth century, it is necessary to survey the nature of intellectual life in the centuries between the explosion of intellectual energy in the sixth century BC and the twelfth century. This will help to place medieval rationalism in perspective.

Interest in rational thinking and science began with the Milesians, who were the first Greeks to show an interest in the function of the natural world. In Greek, the very verb 'to know', $o\tilde{i}\delta\alpha$, has the gerund $i\sigma\tau\omega\rho$, which becomes $i\sigma\tauo\rho i\alpha$, 'history', the act of rational inquiry. In this etymology we see the origin of a conscious use of the mind as an instrument of inquiry and of the desire to harness this use to the effort of understanding all experience — including the physical environment.

That Miletus in the sixth century was both a lively trading centre and a *polis* shaken by frequent changes of government helps to explain why this Greek city provided the necessary climate for the abandonment of a tightly tradition-bound milieu in favour of rationalist modes of thought. We can, I think, put under the rubric 'rationalist' the Milesian thinkers' confident rejection of magical explanations for events in the natural world. They felt a concomitant urge to devise theories based on a need for down-to-earth evidence that could convince those willing to assess it objectively, and to subject their experience to criticism and discussion. Neither of these mental activities had existed before this, even though brilliant technological thinking had already been achieved by the Sumerians and the Egyptians.

Although the Milesians lacked a concept of scientific method and a vocabulary for developing it, their thirst for disinterested inquiry into nature led them to look for causes and to formulate the idea of a basic stuff underlying physical phenomena. It is of less moment that they offered a variety of substances as forming this stuff than that they were able both to imagine its existence and to guard themselves from any temptation to ascribe it, whatever it was, to a supernatural force.

In this study, rational inquiry will be defined as an impersonal way of reacting to human experience in most of its forms. It includes reliance on conscious mental functioning, characterised by courage in asking questions to which traditional answers cannot be applied. By no means am I describing a rigorously scientific approach, but an attitude which impels its holders to go forward in a specific line of questioning relatively unimpeded by traditional or magical explanations, however widely accepted. There is inevitably, in a rationalist temper, a degree of boldness and a general disregard for the accepted solution — the conformist point of view.

Scientific impulse shares some of these attributes but necessarily limits itself to problems relating to natural functioning. Whether concerned with the human body or directed to the planets and stars, the impulse is focused on how and why nature proceeds as it seems to do. Long before a scientific method was deliberated, those who felt this impulse instinctively went after answers and explanations that included the now standard methodological procedures: the quest for causation; the gathering and sifting of relevant data for use in inductive reasoning and the forming of hypotheses; the deductive techniques of logical analysis of the results of such hypothesising and the concomitant dependence on empirical techniques. Measuring, counting and the use of geometric spatial symbols were incorporated quite early; and perhaps most remarkable of all was the ability — or the reaching out for such an ability — to envision and to endure an incomplete supposition or a partial and tentative explanation. These procedures implied a continuous, non-ending incremental search for natural knowledge.

It seems clear that the habit of popular discussion and debate of ideas that became evident in Greek cities in the fifth and sixth centuries had a part to play in the growth of science, especially of abstract theorising about natural causes and their components. The rise of the art and practice of rhetoric contributed greatly to this theorising tendency. The Greeks' passion for argument naturally inclined them towards an increasing awareness of the power of language. New words entered — and altered — the thinking of those reflecting on nature by the mid-fourth century; such new terms as matter, substance and cause made for a dramatic leap in scientific thinking.

Rather than perceiving a rational mood as a curious anomaly arising in unlikely times and places, an anthropological approach suggests that when certain physical and social preconditions exist, this frame of mind appears in some (always comparatively few) men.

The historical fact that an enlightenment age has always been the result of a relatively small group living in a generally unaware society is sometimes overlooked. Just as a tiny minority of scientists actually produce major contributions to science, so do only a very small number of philosophers contribute to significant innovations in conceptual thinking.

A comparative study of the Greek and French enlightenments suggests that several preconditions were present. A basic level of economic security prevailed, allowing at least enough prosperity to ensure an adequate diet and a secure physical environment permitting a degree of health and mental development. Another element upon which a rationalist phase depends is enough political security to ensure freedom from anarchy or constant military attacks. Even better is the kind of political condition that allows men to feel personally involved, however slightly, in government, as for example in the pre-Socratic days when the so-called Tyrants competed for power using speeches appealing to the people for support. I am not here claiming a democratic government is a requisite for rational or scientific thinking, although a connection can be made; but a rationalist mood is only possible when men do not suffer the sense of complete anonymity and of living as passive puppets.

For psychological security, such a period should also possess continuity of custom and a feeling of tradition that is alive and operating, whether in social mores or religion. Without such a background it is difficult to stand aside from experience long enough to question it on any level. There must also be literacy widely enough enjoyed for a number of men to share a questioning, discussion-based, intellectual life. After all, even when men can write, they need an audience of peers. And it is essential, I believe, that this literacy be truly comfortable, so that its possessors can afford to play with words and ideas without having uneasily to husband the former and laboriously construct the latter. The ability to sustain the effort of productive critical thinking and scientific inquiry requires a discipline of education capable of giving the requisite ease and familiarity with language and its uses.

Again, the rationalist requires — or prospers when his society offers — encouragement and regard, however slight. He will think more creatively and with more confidence when he feels that a theory he constructs might be seriously considered. This ambience, as it were, of the rationalist world, is almost universal in an enlightenment period. A sense of competitive energy in the social environment is also requisite: lively minds are attracted to like minds which can offer stimulation, and this leads to an *agon* — a perceived mental challenge that urges men to outdo themselves. The habit of travel is conducive to rationalist activity: an awareness of how others live releases the imagination and loosens the hold of parochial narrowness and prejudice.

Finally, for a rationalist mood to exist for any productive end, some degree of freedom of ideas must exist. Whether it is caused by lack of concern over intellectual movements by the government, or by lack of sufficient political power to oppose a critical rationalist movement, there can be no concerted effort to think effectively, unless some freedom to think and write exists.

The *physikoi* of ancient Greece were not professional scientists; some taught, some were physicians, some statesmen. They practised their *métier* as a craft, but, as they received no financial recompense, they had either to be in other professions or from well-to-do families. Greek *physikoi* believed that their investigations were to be conducted purely for intellectual satisfaction — that knowledge was to be sought for its own sake, neither to gain control over nature nor for fame or financial gain. 'Fortunate is he who engages in inquiry and who observes the ageless order of immortal nature,' Euripides wrote. Seneca, in his *Quaestiones naturales* (III, *praef.*), which were known in the twelfth century, provides a motive for the study of nature. He argued that the intellectual exercise entailed was an aid to living, imparting a sense of courage and a valuable distancing from the slavery of mundane concerns.[1]

To assist us in fully comprehending the gap in scientific interest that stretched into the eleventh century AD from approximately the second century, when science largely disappeared, let us note the steps towards an increasingly wide rejection of rationalist and scientific thinking, in favour of magical and occult thinking, that occurred after the fourth century BC. Pythagoras and his followers had long since blended supernatural thinking with mathematical and empirical studies. Empedocles also divided his attention between developing a theory of the elements and a belief that he himself partook of divinity. And after the fourth century, the art of reading the future by means of the stars was increasingly popular.

Although sceptical attitudes appear even in the pre-Socratics, it is in the fourth and third centuries BC that men were again drawn to various forms of expression of reaction against rationalist and scientific modes of thought. From Antisthenes on, some rallied round the idea that probing nature and stepping back from experience were not only of no real use but were morally unsound. For example, the Cynics of the third century BC reviled ordered, rational thought in favour of a primitive unconsciousness. They rejected mathematics and learning in general, seeing 'virtue' as the supreme value, and promoted moral preaching instead. Like Rousseau, the Cynics connected ethical concerns with a distrust of abstract intellectual effort, and made of their reaction a moral crusade.

The sceptics took a strong stand against dogmatism of any sort, and preferred a position of conscious withholding of belief in any doctrine. Pyrrho, the founder of sceptism, is said to have attained an admirable state of equanimity ($\dot{\alpha}\tau\alpha\rho\alpha\chi\iota\dot{\alpha}$), defined as imperturbability and freedom from disquiet. Later, in the Hellenistic period, there was a shift in emphasis from the goal of suspending belief to those methods which produced such detachment; and these later sceptics emphasised open-minded, continual inquiry.[2]

We are not here reviewing all the forms of reaction to the Greek enlightenment, but among the most significant forms the neoplatonist movement deserves attention. Towards the end of the third century AD, Plotinus, using Plato's myths and metaphors, created the most elegant metaphysical system the ancient world produced. Plotinus' system — a significant anti-intellectual reaction to Greek rationalism — was peculiarly satisfying to many of his contemporaries struggling to maintain sanity in an increasingly fragmented world. His formulations were received with enthusiastic acceptance by the Church fathers and most significantly by Augustine.

The Greek rationalist mood and its achievements gave way to a Christian perspective. This gave a view of existence whose intent was to eliminate the unbearable anxiety of moral contingency and to make of minimal weight the appalling helplessness men felt before it.[3] The brief time when men experienced the sense of possessing some degree of control over their lives (a prerequisite for a rational mood) came to an end by the time Christianity was gathering adherents and forming doctrinal complexities and an institutional framework. The great majority felt largely disenfranchised and quite helpless politically and economically under the imperial rule.

As Dodds has pointed out, a tendency towards mystical experience and the growth of mystical theories was apparent in the second and third centuries AD. Mysticism is clearly one form of response to the increasing difficulties of life in this period. E.R. Dodds writes:

> From a world so impoverished intellectually, so insecure
> materially, so filled with fear and hatred as the world of the third
> century, any path that promised escape must have attracted
> serious minds. . . . The entire culture, pagan as well as Christian,
> was moving into a phase in which religion was to be co-extensive
> with life, and the question of God was to cast its shadow over all
> other human activities.[4]

In this period, men became more absorbed in thinking in religious
terms, and less concerned with the disinterested observation of
natural experience. Philosophy became increasingly a religious
pursuit. The anonymous author of *Hermetic Aesclepius* wrote
that 'Philosophy must be kept free from importunate intellectual
curiosity.'[5]

A stark testament to the disorder of the times is given by Cyprian in
his work *Ad Demetrion*:

> The world today speaks for itself: by the evidence of its decay it
> announces its dissolution. The farmers are vanishing from the
> countryside, commerce from the sea, soldiers from the camps; all
> honesty in business, all justice in the courts, all solidarity in
> friendship, all skill in the arts, all standards in morals — all
> are disappearing.[6]

Prophecies and oracles proliferated in this period. As Dodds points
out, 'The increasing demand for oracles . . . reflects an increasing
insecurity of the times.'[7]

By the sixth century, although Boethius and Martius Cappella
spent their energies on transmitting what they could of the earlier
thought, the few literate men in Europe, nearly all of them
ecclesiastics, had little time and less incentive to attempt any forays
into scientific inquiry, or indeed into any form of objective
questioning of reality.

Beryl Smalley points out that the fifth to the ninth centuries were
largely concerned with the collection of minutiae and encyclopaedic
lore. She refers to this as a decadent period where 'erudition', the
accumulation of curious and marvellous facts, had become more
interesting than the investigation of natural laws. '. . . The pagan
learning which St. Augustine recommended could not include
scientific method; he could only insist on the best training that the
schools of rhetoric could supply. . . .'[8] Isidore of Seville's *Etymologia*

exemplifies this preoccupation: his work transmitted items of Greek science embedded in a pudding of myth, popular lore and historical fact.

Why are periods of even partial enlightenment so rare? And why do they tend to weaken and collapse? Is it because the preconditions for them have so rarely been met, or is there some other reason? Clearly, the combination of favourable economic, political and intellectual conditions has indeed been rare and then only of short duration. There is something in the human psyche that tends to undermine an objective, critical cast of mind after a time; sceptics are most often converted to, or succeeded by, 'believers' — adopting attitudes of acquiescence in the prevailing orthodoxy. One theory explains this phenomenon by proposing that the cerebral cortex, the only portion of the brain capable at all of disinterested rational thought, can rarely contend successfully with the other, older, less evolved portions. These are concerned only with survival mechanisms or with clinging to the comfort of animal group behaviour. Belief, for the Greeks, meant to trust someone or some aspect of tradition which had authority behind it. Later, belief came to include doctrines concerning the spiritual, the transcendent — formulations invoking spiritual or supernatural power. Since it is the many, not the few, who create and transmit tradition, it is easy to see how most men will retreat to tradition sooner or later, more quickly and completely when times are uncertain and living becomes more difficult.

To sum up, the continuing and increasingly adverse reaction to Greek science and rationalist attitudes from Aristotle's day to the late eleventh century can be traced to the growing unease and anxiety that men experienced in the disintegrating world of war, anarchy and tribalism that followed the relatively secure and psychologically free world of the Greek *polis* that preceded it. When the early Christian cult was transformed into a political institution, the incentives for an open probing into all kinds of experience absolutely ceased to exist. And although random snippets of scientific' thinking were collected and handed on between Augustine's life (d. 430) and Berengar's in the late eleventh century, they were never widely read or indeed understood sufficiently to reawaken this evanescent and fragile mood — until the twelfth century.

For a short time in the twelfth century, Western Europe permitted men to indulge in a kind of speculative thought about the universe — about society, about history, about the relation between the sexes, even about the Church. Such reflection was characterised by an objective approach, analytical and capable of courageous inquiry into everything and anything connected with their world.

But creative rational thinking, with some notable exceptions, virtually dies after Aristotle and is replaced by a variety of belief systems, magical and philosophical, which seek to banish the sense of helplessness and uncertainty contingent on the eroding of all traditional forms; tradition here is a complex of codified reactions to experience sanctified by the passage of time. The effort of rational thinking, which presupposes an optimistic confidence about this life's possibilities, ceased to be worth making. And the world moved from an active concern for worldly happiness and contentment to an obsession with other-worldly 'salvation'. Already by the eleventh century there had been brave attempts made by medieval men to fashion a methodical system for investigating natural phenomena, to apply logic to the body of writing — the *auctores* — that constituted their entire source of information on all subjects, from Christian metaphysics to medicine. Travelling to foreign centres of non-Latin culture such as Toledo and Sicily, they taught themselves Arabic the better to uncover new ideas and approaches to the world in which they lived. Writing discursive treatises on science or society, some men found the strength to stand back from the hitherto fearful and mysterious world and apply a trained, critical intellect to the pressing problems of the world as it was.

A growing preoccupation with political and social tensions brought this mood to an end as the twelfth century drew to a close and the burgeoning power and scope of institutional development had a powerful effect on intellectual life. The best minds were trained to run the increasingly effective political institutions or for teaching theology, a metaphysical structure of systematic thought that reached its zenith a century later. It is no accident that the new mode of thinking was accompanied by a conservative religious revolution, for precisely the same development occurred in both Islamic and Jewish thought at that time.

The *Timaeus* and Scientific Inquiry

In almost every medieval library of any importance there was a copy of the incomplete Chalcidius Latin translation of the *Timaeus* together with commentaries, fragments and summaries by Chalcidius, Cicero, Macrobius, Galen, Seneca and others.[9] It was the only work of Plato that Europe knew and the only one, too, that the Arabs, who had available the complete Platonic corpus, chose to translate from the ninth century on. To medieval thinkers, then, Plato meant the *Timaeus*, but a *Timaeus* somewhat altered from the original text; for in late antiquity this dialogue was singled out for special treatment by a school of philosophers influenced by oriental ideas. The most famous of these thinkers were Plotinus and his followers, such as Proclus and Porphyry. It was through their medium that Augustine, the most potent of medieval influences, learned Platonic thought. For medieval men, Augustine's admiration of Plato provided a powerful incentive for welcoming the *Timaeus*, not because he paid specific attention to that work, but because much of his own philosophical programme was based on the Platonic emphasis on rational knowledge.[10] This is not to say that he ignored the *Timaeus*, for he expressed the belief that 'The Platonic doctrine of a universe "formed by God" was not incompatible with Christian dogma',[11] a belief to which we will refer again.

Much has been written on the subject of the influence of the form of the Platonic tradition initiated by Plotinus. In certain respects it had a deleterious effect on the development of science in the middle ages; it stressed an antithesis between spirit and matter and encouraged an asceticism which implied a strong denigration of the value of the senses. Such an attitude was bound to discourage the empirical study of natural phenomena. Augustine himself was drawn in this direction, so deeply sympathetic to the Christian sensibility, and helped to reinforce the tendency of his time to mistrust the senses and knowledge based upon them. In describing the various temptations that plagued him, Augustine wrote:

> For besides that concupiscence of the flesh ... the soul hath, through the same senses of the body, a certain vain and curious desire, veiled under the title of knowledge and learning, not of delighting in the flesh but of making experiments through the flesh. The seat whereof being in the appetite of knowledge, and sight being the sense chiefly used for attaining knowledge, it is in Divine language called the lust of the eyes [*concupiscentia oculorum*].[12]

Hence it would seem that for a good Christian, scientific research would be thought of as an unsavoury occupation. This rather curious but quite logical objection to the empirical approach of knowledge was, in fact, reinforced in the *Timaeus* by Plato's declared preference for mathematical and deductive proof over empirical evidence as being less uncertain and more amenable to validation. This is but one of the ways in which the *Timaeus* was peculiarly adaptable to medieval sensibilities.

The *Timaeus* satisfied the newly experienced need for a rational explanation of the universe because of its logical account of creation. This account was such as to allow medieval Christians to accept it, with some adjustments, as congruous with Genesis. For the middle ages, 'Plato was not the logician nor the philosopher of love nor the author of the *Republic*. He was, next to Moses, the great monotheistic cosmogonist, the philosopher of creation . . .'[13] And it is an irony of history that this great moral philosopher should become the patron saint of medieval science.

Much has been made of Plato's influence on medieval minds, yet as Raymond Klibansky reminds us, much remains to be learned. The twelfth-century Platonist writings are notably various: Brian Stock and Winthrop Weatherbee have examined the effect of Platonic tradition on twelfth-century poetry and Tullio Gregory and Richard Lemay have added to our understanding of its effect on philosophical and theoretical thought in this period. The rich accretions of Hermetic and astrological material have been studied along with the older Plotinian interpretations and the whole complicated orchestration of these various themes has received minute attention.[14] Moreover, in this diversity of Platonic writings, a strongly imaginative quality is often present. Indeed, as Peter Dronke says:

> They are achievements not only of the rational intellect but of the fictive imagination. Their cosmological insights are nourished by imaginative springs as much as by the disciplined sources of abstract thinking. Theirs is a realm where sacred visions and profane myth can combine with analytic thought, poetic fantasy with physical and metaphysical speculation. In terms of scholarship it is a realm which, because it is at the borders of several genres, is still in many ways a neglected one.[15]

The genre of these twelfth-century Platonic writings that might be classified as cosmological or scientific has yet to be fully explored. Scholars have tended to focus on the mystical vein in the Plotinian or neoplatonic tradition, ignoring a fecund source of intellectual development; this has had the effect of turning medievalists exclusively towards metaphysical problems — at the expense of such a rational problem as an objective interest in nature.

The *Timaeus*, we should keep in mind, is the only work of Plato that has had an uninterrupted existence. The work spawned an enormous progeny of commentaries beginning with those of Plato's students and surely not ending with this study some 2300 years later. Indeed, the rich strand of western thought we often refer to as the Platonic tradition can be seen as largely composed of the body of writing deriving from the *Timaeus* alone of Plato's voluminous work. For after the closing of the Academy, the entire corpus of his writings would have completely disappeared in the West (where Greek ceased to be spoken) if Chalcidius had not decided — towards the end of the third century AD — to translate and gloss the *Timaeus* in Latin. It was this translation that survived in an incomplete form through the succeeding 1200 years, and it was this version of the work that the western world knew until Ficino revived Plato's Academy in the late fifteenth century.[16]

In the first half of the twelfth century a number of men in Western Europe — such philosophers as Adelard of Bath, Hugh of St Victor, Thierry of Chartres, Peter Abelard and William of Conches — saw in the *Timaeus* an account of the creation of the world quite different from that in Genesis, finding in it an approach to nature that gave them compelling reason for engaging in a sustained investigation of the cosmos.[17] I have already suggested that a genuine scientific revolution took place at this time which led to a conscious, articulated programme of theoretical and methodological science — a preparation without which no serious science could come.[18] This revolution, one manifestation of a strong rationalist impulse in the early twelfth century, produced the desire to formulate and explore questions concerning natural phenomena, applying logic and experience.

The view of R.W. Southern that the twelfth-century *physici* were far from possessing a genuine understanding of science and were simply repeating ancient clichés about reason that go back to the watered-down version of Aristotle transmitted through Boethius is, I think, based on a concept of science that is confined to its practice, that is, to making discoveries of a specific nature or of a general theory, such as Einstein's theory of relativity. If, however, we adopt a definition of scientific thinking which embraces a perception of the value of objective investigation of the workings of nature, a serious effort to outline a *modus operandi* for a formal discipline of such investigation, and finally, a strong sense of the value of such an enterprise for the benefit of mankind, we are, I believe, on firm ground. For such imaginative playing with the notion of *ratio* was a precious contribution to western thought in the middle ages; and though it gave way to something quite different as the century ended, the texts incorporating it were absorbed by Grosseteste and Roger Bacon a century later and by generations of readers in the succeeding three centuries.[19]

The thrust of my argument is markedly different from that of the medievalists mentioned above: that William of Conches and others found in the *Timaeus* both an idea of science and an incentive for recommending its pursuit. This concept of science involved the development of a methodology, a compact, interconnected constellation of ideas which helped these men to formulate a precise notion of what natural philosophy could be. These ideas were the principle of causality; the association of the idea of process with nature; the doctrine of primal matter; the mathematical structure underlying the elements and their permutations; the empirical basis for scientific inquiry which combines deductive reasoning, induction and the forming of hypotheses; all while remaining receptive to the painful uncertainty that merely probable knowledge entails.

The motive for engaging in science was of great significance for these thinkers; they were aware that such pursuit was a serious matter not so much because of a superstitious fear of nature as a realistic fear of the danger that the disinterested investigation of nature — of God's creation — could have for a medieval Christian. But in the twelfth-century reading of the *Timaeus*, the conclusion drawn was that one should use one's intelligence to study the cosmos, increasing one's understanding of all aspects of its functioning. This knowledge or *scientia* does not exist in a vacuum, but has both practical and ethical implications. William saw science as a legitimate extension of *politica* and *ethica* and consonant with Christian tenets.

Literacy and the New Men

That there was great interest in the *Timaeus* in the early decades of the twelfth century we know from many sources, but why then? One consequence of the increasing prosperity and efficient government in Western Europe at this period was the appearance of a lay and lively intellectual group in England and France calling themselves *moderni*.[20] These men gathered in informal study groups in the rising towns and acquainted themselves with Aristotle's logic, Latin literature and rhetoric, Greek and Arab medicine. Teachers found a ready audience among young men ambitious to train themselves for the new posts and professions opening up in the royal courts as well as in bustling commercial towns.

Previously, literacy was largely limited to the clergy, whose exclusive control of education filled the needs of a simple feudal society. At this time, however, townsmen benefited from a new sense of physical security; fresh energies were released for purely secular ends: the continuing expansion of urban commerce, the consequent elaboration of banking techniques and the resulting political development both within the large towns and the western kingdoms. These changes, together with the increasing specialisation of the movement toward a centralised and bureaucratically administered government, created a professional class requiring literacy and special training — a requisite degree of education that stimulated the desire to acquire a trained intellect, a necessary tool for professional life.

For the first time since antiquity western societies were able to encourage and support an intellectual class — a prerequisite at any time for sustained scientific advance.[21] The new attention paid to education and to the value of the trained mind produced confidence in the mind's powers, and, inevitably, a new questioning mood, an intellectual arrogance if you will, that intensified a belief in rationality and the applicability of this principle to all kinds of human concerns.

Attendant on this mood was a sharpened appetite for any writings — ancient or contemporary — that supplied either theory or practice, information and speculation about nature and its workings.[22] Along with a smattering of Greek science from early Latin sources and recent Latin translations from Greek and Arabic sources, the intellectually aware 'modern men' read the *Timaeus* with interest. There are many expressions of deep admiration for Plato at this time. William calls Plato 'of all philosophers the wisest'.[23] Adelard of Bath calls him 'my friend, Plato';[24] 'the extraordinary arcane Plato', says Robert of Melun;[25] and 'this [philosopher] of the Academicians the divine, sainted Plato, chief of the philosophers', claims John of Salisbury.[26] An anonymous writer of the day wrote that to read the *Timaeus* is to penetrate into the secrets of nature and truth.[27] In his *Glosae super Macrobius* William of Conches says that for him Plato is far greater than Aristotle — a more subtle thinker. One of the most popular of the *moderni*, William wrote a guide to the *Timaeus* which was widely circulated in Europe for three hundred years and was still read in Ficino's time.[28]

With his awareness of the exciting possibilities for new applications of the trained intellect, William was in a singular position to absorb Plato's view of the value of a study of nature. Training in logic — in reasoning processes and techniques — that had become a part of secular education in the new cathedral schools beginning to flourish in the towns fostered this sort of intellectual adventurousness. By the 1120s, a generation had submitted to the rigorous training that the art of dialectic demanded. This training instilled in those who mastered it a sense of intellectual control, an awareness that dialectic, the ability to reason consciously and effectively, was a useful and splendid skill. The 'new men' prided themselves on their bold, daring thought. And to look at nature objectively, to conceive of science after so many centuries of fear and superstitious response, was very daring indeed. Dialectic was seen, then, not as an esoteric and separate discipline, but as an indispensable part of the proper study of the Latin language and literature.

Rhetoric and *Ratio*

Rhetoric in the twelfth century was not studied for ornamentation or persuasion merely, but was perceived to be, as William of Conches said, a vital part of the pursuit of *eloquentia* — a necessary aspect of the discipline to gain a confident control of language. Such control was the *sine qua non* of acquiring *ratio* — a technique of reasoning for a specific purpose, such as the study of natural science. For this use of rhetoric, a mechanism whereby language functions as a tool in intellect, was taken from classical sources but used in an original manner in the early twelfth century. Thierry of Chartres sees clearly the value to the serious thinker of the study of grammar and rhetoric,[29] and Hugh of St Victor thinks of the study of dialectic as a rational discipline along with them. Hugh wrote that the nature of argument itself should be considered first:

> Once this was known, then they [the ancients who perfected the technique of argumentation] could also know whether the results discovered by argument were truly held. Hence, skill in the discipline of logic began — that discipline which provides ways of distinguishing between modes of argument and the trains of

reasoning themselves, so that it can be known which trains of reasoning are sometimes true, sometimes false, and which never false . . . It is logic which ought to be read first by those beginning the study of philosophy, for it teaches the nature of words and concepts, without both of which no treatises of philosophy can be explained rationally . . . [There are two senses or kinds of logic] rational logic, which is called argumentative, contains dialectic and rhetoric. Linguistic logic stands as genus to grammar, dialectic and rhetoric.[30]

William of Conches, a celebrated teacher as well as writer, was known as one of the greatest *grammatici* of his day; he had a command of the techniques of literary exegesis which helped him to read the *Timaeus* as he read Virgil — sensitively and accurately. Williams says that:

> such is the order of learning, that, because all things are learned through eloquence, that must be taught first. Eloquence has three parts: to write correctly . . . which *grammatica* deals with; to prove what has to be proven, which *dialectica* teaches; and to ornament . . . sentences which *rhetorica* provides. Therefore we begin with grammar, then dialectic, and afterwards, rhetoric. Having been instructed in these disciplines and, as it were, fortified with arms, we must then proceed to the study of philosophy.[31]

Twelfth-century *grammatici* were skilled in the use of rhetorical tropes and figurative devices such as allegory, symbol and metaphor. William says, 'When philosophers speak of a world soul, they are moving in the direction of myth and metaphor, as Plato did in the *Timaeus.*'[32] Peter Abelard, a poet as well as a philosopher, discussing the notion of a world possessing conscious intellectual powers, writes that it is clear than when *anima mundi* is spoken of by philosophers, the words must be taken as metaphor (*per involucrum*); '. . . otherwise we should have to censure Plato, the greatest of philosophers, as the greatest of fools.' What, Abelard asks, is more ridiculous than to think of the entire world as a single rational animal — unless the meaning is extended *per integumentum*?[33]

Integumentum is the term used for the outer sense of a passage of a poem cunningly designed by the artist to reveal effectively only to the adroit reader the carefully hidden inner meaning, the true significance of an important idea. Bernard Silvestris defines *integumentum* as a kind of demonstration under the category of narrative fable involving the intellect, sometimes called *involucrum*,[34] whereas William writes of the *Timaeus*, 'The metaphor having been expounded, let us come to the letter', fully aware of the artistry of this highly wrought literary masterwork. In understandable impatience with those who are unwilling to deal with the dimension of metaphor, William writes 'Underlings [*garciones*], intent on chatter and ignorant of any philosophy, and for that reason, unaware of the significance of the parables [*integumenta*] and ashamed to admit their ignorance, seeking solace for their own incapacity, they say that it is immoral to explicate such matters.'[35] He was alert always to suggestive words and phrases that might be clues leading the reader towards a cumulative power and clarity of meaning by somewhat circuitous paths. Dante, a century later, wrote that 'Plato insinuates a great deal in his works through his use of metaphor; for he saw much through the light of intellect which he was unable to express in ordinary discourse.'[36]

William is interested in nature, its structure and operations; he speaks of Plato's finding the universe rational in its design and function.[37] Before the twelfth century, nature — post-lapsarian nature — had been felt to be hostile to man, evoking fear and wonder. George Henderson writes, 'In the early middle ages ... the omnipresent uncontrollable forces of nature were inevitably imagined in terms of active malignant intelligences, enemies of God and men.'[38] *Natura* was sometimes reduced to a mere framework for practical use, or it was used symbolically as a veil through which a spiritual reality could be glimpsed. Hugh of St Victor defines *physica*, the study of natural things: '. . . it searches out and considers the causes of things as found in their effects, and the effects as derived from certain causes.'[39]

A belief in the basic orderliness or regularity of the cosmos is expressed in the concept of natural causation. It is this concept, repeatedly stated and also implied in the *Timaeus*, that gave the *moderni* their faith in the possibility of a discipline of science. William of Conches, absorbing Plato's notion of *physis* — natural phenomena possessed of a transient existence — writes that nature or the world, is that which is born . . . and nothing is born or has a beginning without a cause [*sine causa*]; hence if there was no cause, or principle of causation, there could be no world.[40] He goes on to assert that the world is a generated thing because it is produced or made; that nature is corporeal, composed of diverse elements and, hence, an artifact; and finally, that the world consists of corporeal things that are visible and tangible.[41] Science as possible, as conceivable, was inferred from the notion of the rationality of nature. The mind trained in logic is adept in science; Hugh of St Victor saw that rules for reasoning helped to provide a science of language which could assist scientific inquiry. Logic, 'an art of arts, a science of sciences', was a rational discipline:

> Because logic and mathematics are prior to *physica* [natural science] in the order of learning and serve *physica* . . . as tools . . . it was necessary that these two sciences base their considerations . . . upon reason alone . . . and with reason to lead them they descend into the physical order [i.e. the sensible world].[42]

Allied to the systematic use of deductive reasoning was Plato's reliance on mathematical principles; the geometrical foundation of the elements of underlying natural phenomena.[43] Thierry of Chartres writes, '. . . but the creation of numbers is the creation of [natural] things',[44] and William of Conches says, 'Plato, like Pythagoras, knew the greatest perfection to be in numbers, since it is not possible that anything created exists without number.'[45]

The Medieval Perception of Plato's Matter

In the history of science, Plato has traditionally had a bad press in comparison with Aristotle. Recently, however, there are signs of a change, for with the wide dispersal of understanding of contemporary physics and chemistry among writers in this area, we are hearing more about Plato's contribution and considerably less about the beneficence of Aristotle's influence on the early development of science. The concept 'matter', ὑλή, was Plato's, as was the term element. στοιχεῖον is a component of nature, the lowest divisible state where reason is able to perceive order.[46]

Perhaps the most germinal of all Plato's ideas in the *Timaeus* is the suggestion that the basic constituents of the four elements are geometric in form, solid bodies composed of triangles. The idea that each element has a particular atomic, geometric structure which assigns a mathematical construction to everything in the universe was immensely suggestive to the twelfth-century reader.[47] William says:

After he [Plato] shows the basic material of the world, that is, the four elements, and why four have been created and not fewer, he explains how the world has been constructed from such matter, constructed in such a way that no matter exists beyond it.[48]

William here implies that the world is purely material; and Plato's emphasis on the very existence of primal stuff that is the basis of all natural phenomena is of itself pregnant with possibilities for science, and was so felt by the *moderni*. William wonders about these elements: What is their structure? Can they be seen? divided?[49] The *moderni*, sometimes called *physici*, who were beginning to concern themselves with natural philosophy, carefully considered Plato's description of the disordered and unproportioned elements that were in a state of chaos before the god, the ordering intelligence, created our cosmos; after this act the shapeless elements were assigned a mathematical form of shape and number. The treatment of the elements in the *Timaeus*, especially the fact that they were composed of four substances, was for the medieval mind peculiarly challenging; it seemed to impel readers to envisage a discipline of natural science even without the conceptual framework of which it was only a part.

It is worth stressing that the *Timaeus*'s emphasis on νοῦς, mind or intelligence, as the underlying factor of the created world, of nature, is not only the basic element in the twelfth-century aesthetic appreciation of the natural world, but is also the *sine qua non* of the entire humanist movement or 'renaissance' of the period. For it is precisely this idea, or ideal, if you will, of a governing, reasoning order pervading the universe and the renewed confidence that awareness of this ideal brings, that was needed to ignite the so-easily-extinguished spark of belief in the human capacity for development.

Medieval Empiricism and the *Timaeus*

William points out that for Plato, observation is a most useful tool for the scientist. It is not possible to do without it, for anyone studying natural phenomena (*de re universa*) cannot truly investigate except through observation.[50] For Plato, experience led to the acquiring of an appropriate skill, *techne*, or what William of Conches called *ars*, which combined practical skill and theoretical knowledge. William holds that the discipline of science (*physiea*) consists in the investigation of natural phenomena according to a variety of approaches: through mathematics, abstract thought or theorising, and reasoning that follows from observations of types of phenomena (*ad occulum per formas et descriptiones*). But when these approaches are combined — i.e. the mathematical, the logical or deductive type of reasoning and the empirical — the results compare most favourably with any one of the approaches alone.[51] William believes that whoever is not inquiring is not concerned to investigate the universe, and is not a true philosopher. To do this properly involves a dependence upon observation; learning by direct experience was seen to be part of a genuine scientific methodology.[52]

William did not, however, think of Plato's empirical approach as implying a closed structure of thought or procedure. He sees Plato's use of sense-data as a necessary component — in its inevitable imperfection, provisionality, unverifiability — of any investigation of nature, even though empirical knowledge can never give us the degree of certainty that mathematical truths can. Our senses are irrational and hence somewhat unsatisfactory, William believes, though they are helpful and necessary for gaining understanding of nature.

An important element in this methodology was the forming of hypotheses based on experience and William makes frequent use of this procedure. The principle of induction was also grasped by the *Timaeus*'s twelfth-century readers. In forming hypotheses one collected and interpreted natural evidence (*hoc probat*) that supported the theory being formulated. Hypothesising was seen as a serious activity for the scientist: one dealt with 'proofs', but in so doing one was also allowed an element of uncertainty, for that allows the forming of hypotheses.[53] A degree of uncertainty is, as it were, built into the activity of gaining knowledge of nature, for what is alive must inevitably grow and decay. Adelard of Bath, too, fully grasped the tentative, uncertain character of empirical data when he agreed with Plato's view that the senses were irrational.[54] William says that what exists is that which is born (*gignitur*) and decays and it is possible to investigate such natural phenomena by means of reasoning. But there is necessarily room for doubt or error in such investigating because this sort of knowledge can only be incomplete and tentative. William gives us an example of the problematic aspect of scientific study — when we observe a stick in water, it seems to be broken although we know it to be whole. The perishability of all living things is a given in nature, but since extinction is literally incomplete — something does remain since primordal matter is necessarily indestructible — there is always a continuing element, a residue. William of Conches believes in the paradoxical aspect of nature that somehow combines continual change with a thread of continuity. Again, there is an irreducible element of chance, a randomness that co-exists with the overall rationality of nature.[55]

Yet, though chance must be allowed for, the builder of hypotheses, in his investigations of natural process, keeps in mind the idea of probability, an idea that is integral to any real science. Plato had come to see that '. . . there can be, strictly speaking, no such thing as knowledge of nature — only educated guesses, versimilitudes, plausibilities', Gregory Vlastos writes.[56] William of Conches everywhere shows his understanding of this: Plato, he is aware, continually suggests the contrast between the *paradeigma*, the pattern or model of moral excellence and also (though on a lower plane) of mathematical and logical truths which is always certain and reliable, and the understanding of nature, which can only be incomplete and tentative: ἐὶκοτα μυθον, 'a likely story'.[57] The often reiterated dichotomy between the timeless, irrefutable and permanent nature of ethical truths and the uncertain, incomplete nature of science was readily perceived by the twelfth-century readers of the *Timaeus*.

Faith and Science

The twelfth-century *physici* found problems in harmonising Plato's account of the creation of the world with Genesis; we can imagine their dismay on reading in the beginning of the *Timaeus*

> . . . Timaeus . . . who knows more about astronomy than the rest of us, and who has devoted himself particularly to studying the nature of the universe, should speak first and, starting with the origin of the cosmic system, bring the story down to man.[59]

Although some Christian readers of the *Timaeus* were able easily to accommodate the work to their religion, others were troubled by what they saw as inconsistencies. Those who defended Plato's account as not inconsistent with Christian belief championed him vigorously.[60]

The *physici* thought that science and Christianity were more than compatible, that they were, in fact, complementary. Certainly, questions of heresy did arise and William himself became entangled in the problem of Plato's relation to Christianity. In the early twelfth century it was still possible for a broad latitude of positions regarding theological questions to be offered for discussion. Indeed, the new interest in hermeneutics encouraged a variety of possibilities for consideration.[61]

The wide spectrum of ideas such as those of a Berengar of Tours, a Roscellinus and even a Peter Abelard was still conceivable before 1150. It should be kept in mind that such positions or suggestions were not seen by their progenitors as heretical or at all antithetical to Christian doctrine; we have statements to that effect by all these men — most notably by Abelard and William of Conches, both of whom faced opposition by their ecclesiastical peers. William defends his Greek master and accuses Plato's detractors of failing to perceive Plato's method. William comes to Plato's view of the manner in which God assigned human souls to particular stars. 'Because', he stated indignantly:

> someone reads the passage quite literally, they say that Plato teaches heresy. . . . Yet if anyone got to know not Plato's actual words so much as their sense, he would find not so much heresy as metaphors that carefully conceal the deepest philosophical concepts. As for us, we are careful only to reveal Plato himself.[62]

In the early part of the twelfth century there was a degree of intellectual suppleness that allowed men to stand back from experience, to resist the natural impulse to seek certainties and to attempt a degree of objectivity. After 1150 they turned to system building and devoted their intellectual energies to putting an end to, or at least reducing, the anxiety attendant upon contending with the inevitable uncertainties of unstructured objective inquiry. With the assimilation of the entire corpus of Aristotelian science which provided answers to questions on every aspect of nature (as the medieval philosophers thought) and with the rapid expansion and elaboration of bureaucratic government by kings and popes and of secular education — increasingly available in the nascent universities that appear under the aegis of the Church around 1200 — the temptation to create and expand patterns of thought increased greatly. Hence the new scholastics focused their considerable intellectual powers on giving shape and order to the various and often bewilderingly contradictory statements concerning the received assumptions about God, man and the cosmos. A rich theology gradually emerged greatly aided by the new Aristotle and also by the new commentaries on Roman law. By the thirteenth century, although some men made genuine efforts to work in science, the old rationalist, creative drive of the *moderni* was largely tamed and, as it were, domesticated, to serve the ends of the vastly growing powers of the Church and temporal monarchy.

The Social Implications of the *Timaeus*

William saw the author of the *Timaeus* as a moralist, theologian, mathematician and rationalist. To paraphrase — in this work (the *Timaeus*), there is contained something of all aspects of philosophy: something concerning the practice of justice, concerning God's purpose in creating the world, the four elements, the creation of living things and of primordial matter. William states that Plato begins the *Timaeus* by treating of right, or justice, that his recapitulating the earlier work, the *Republic*, shows his intention to illustrate the connection between moral law and natural justice, both of which are based on *ratio*, on reason.[63] Since God's plan operates under the rational governing principle of order, men can, and should, inquire into nature using the principle of causation and a disciplined mind.[64] William defines science as the study of the ways in which the four elements and the creation of living things derive from primordial matter. He adds this account of *physica* to his list of subjects — *politica*, *economicus*, *ethica* and *theologica* — that Socrates deals with in the *Timaeus* and concludes that all these arts are treated together in this work with the glorious result of '*hoc totum opus platonicum magne perfectionis esse constitutum enim de tota philosophia.*'[65]

A question arises: Does William of Conches in his reading of the *Timaeus* discern Plato's intention in that so controversial work? In his adumbration of a philosophy that combines an alertness to the value of inquiry *de rerum natura* with an emphasis on the centrality of ethical concerns, are William and his small group of contemporaries divining, in fact, the original import of this intricate literary masterwork? To this reader, is seems very possible: for William's commentary presents a collection of propositions that add up to a thesis — a philosophical position that is at once rational and simple. For William, the *Timaeus* suggested that man is an imperfect, unfinished part of the existing rational order we call the cosmos, nature. There is, however, some degree of perfection present in the constituent parts of the universe, and in some fashion an element of chance or randomness interpenetrates with the overall rationally designed framework. The very fact that everything in nature is subject to growth and decay — 'perpetual perishing' — is an imperfection, but an inescapable one: William's *genituram* (Plato's *gignomenon*), the factor of change or perishability, is inherent in the elements of which nature is composed.

Man is himself an imperfect creature, subject to the process without which nature cannot function. It is, however, God who planned that this be so. The rational Creator also planned that underlying the constituent elements lies a primordial substance that cannot be seen but always must exist as the basis of all created things. Matter, then, something constructed of rational, mathematical form, gives man proof that the cosmos is, at bottom, a rational construction which we natural beings, participating necessarily in the imperfect and transitory aspects of all things, can utilise through our possession of intellects capable of rational thought.

Since, then, the universe and the mind of man are connected, man will profit from engaging in the discipline of science, knowledge of which is one of man's highest privileges, and he will profit, too, from using his power more fully to explore and understand himself. The invention of science as a concept yoked to ethical considerations in the secular world was an innovation of this period. William asks what is the greatest satisfaction in engaging in philosophical study and concludes that the satisfaction lies in its ability to assist us in finding our way toward a greater species of humankind. William says that Plato connects natural order or justice with moral order and the two are always to be seen in a reciprocal relation. The orderly, rational universe and the moral world of men in society are mirror images of each other.[66] All metaphors of immortality, perfection and forms or ideas in the Greek sense of the word are there to reinforce this twofold, this double unity. The enlargement of the pursuit of natural justice for the sake of a continuing reform and enlightenment of man in society to include increasing the sum of knowledge of nature provided medieval Europe with an impeccable motive for engaging in the discipline of science. It is, perhaps, pertinent here to remember that in the twelfth century, as in the seventeenth, both natural and ethical philosophy could be, and indeed usually were, seen as aspects of one inquiry.

Finally, we can admire the imaginative force required freshly to comprehend the *Timaeus* — a brave attempt to extricate the medieval mind from the rigid clasp of a metaphysical and mystical Platonism or, more accurately, neoplatonism. It is an irony of history that the single work of the classical Greek age that most profoundly influenced the mystical tradition in the West was, for a brief period in the middle ages, interpreted as a rationalist document whose purpose was to awaken in the reader an interest in the cosmos as it is, and in a method, and, more important, a motive, for exploiting this interest.

For two millennia, Plato's readers have been reluctant to entertain such a reading of the work and have much preferred a mystical version — one, since the early centuries of our era, consonant with the Christian metaphysical tradition. William of Conches and the other thinkers of his group made of the *Timaeus* instead a rationalist fusion of science and ethics — a reading that only today can again be contemplated.

Notes*

1. For further details on the transmission of Greek science to the middle ages, see Marshall Clagett, *Greek Science in Antiquity* (New York, 1963), pp. 180–205.
2. For a discussion of the modulations of early scepticism, see David Sedley, 'The Motivation of Greek Skepticism', in *The Skeptical Tradition*, Myles Burnyeat (ed.) (Berkeley, 1983), pp. 9–28.
3. There was in this period, as Dodds mentions, a 'wave of pessimism that swept over the West'. E.R. Dodds, *Pagan and Christian in an Age of Anxiety* (Cambridge, 1965), p. 18.
4. Dodds, pp. 100–1.
5. Dodds, p. 92, fn. 4. Augustine says, 'Thus men proceed to investigate the phenomena of nature — the part of nature external to us — though the knowledge is of no value to them; for they wish to know simply for the sake of knowing.' *Confessions* X, 35.
6. Dodds, p. 12.
7. Dodds, p. 57.
8. Beryl Smalley, *The Study of the Bible in the Middle Ages* (Notre Dame, 1964), p. 16.
9. Raymond Klibansky, *The Continuity of the Platonic Tradition during the Middle Ages* (London, 1950), p. 23. Raymond Klibansky says, 'Although these facts are well known, their significance for the history of ideas has perhaps not been sufficiently grasped by historians . . . [its] rational exposition of creation was . . . the starting point and guide for the first groping efforts towards a scientific cosmology.' p. 28.
10. Etienne Gilson, *Reason and Revelation in the Middle Ages* (New York, 1938), p. 22. For a good account of Augustine's exposure to neoplatonism, see Peter Brown, *Augustine of Hippo* (Berkeley, 1967), p. 88 ff.
11. Klibansky, p. 23, cf. Aquinas' opinion that Augustine went along with Platonic tradition as far as he possibly could. (See *Summa Theologica*, I, 84, art. 5, Answer.)
12. St Augustine, *Confessions*, X, trans. Edward B. Pusey (New York, 1957), p. 205.
13. C.S. Lewis, *The Discarded Image* (Cambridge, 1964), p. 52.
14. See Raymond Klibansky, *The Continuity of the Platonic Tradition during the Middle Ages* (London, 1939). Also see Brian Stock, *Myth and Science in the Twelfth Century: A Study of Bernard Silvester* (Princeton, 1972); Tullio Gregory, *Anima Mundi: La Filosofia di Guglielmo De Conches e La Scula Di Chartres* (Firenze, 1955), and *Platonismo medievale* (Firenze, 1958); Richard Lemay, *Abu M'shar and Latin Aristotelianism in the Twelfth Century* (Beirut, 1962); Peter Dronke, 'New

* I have aimed in my translations for both fidelity to the literal sense of the text and a style that can most easily reach the modern reader. I have resorted to an occasional paraphrase as preferable to a strictly verbatim English.

Approaches to the School of Chartres', in *Anuario de estudios medievales* (Barcelona, 1969); N.M. Häring, 'The Creation and Creator of the World, According to Thierry of Chartres and Clarenbaldus of Arras', in *Archives d'his. doct. et litt. du moyen âge* 22 (1955), pp. 137–216; *Commentaries on Boethius* by Thierry of Chartres and his School, edited with introduction by N.M. Håring (Toronto, 1971); Edouard Jeauneau, 'Note sur l'école de Chartres', in *Studi medievali* (1964), pp. 1–45 and 'Quelque aspects du platonisme de Thierry de Chartres', in Association Guillaume Budé, *Congrès de Tours* etc. (Paris, 1954), pp. 289–92; M.D. Chenu, 'La Théologie au douzième siècle', in *Etudes de philosophie medievale* 45 (Paris, 1957), English translation by J. Taylor and L.K. Little (Chicago, 1968); 'La Nouvelle idée de nature et de savoir scientifique du XIIe siècle' by Tullio Gregory, in *The Cultural Context of Medieval Learning*, J.E. Murdoch and E.D. Sylla (eds) (Dordrecht, 1975), pp. 192–218.

15. Peter Dronke, *Fabula: Explorations into the Uses of Myth in Medieval Platonism* (Leiden, 1974), introduction, p. 1.

16. For a full account of the dispersion of the Chalcidius translation during the middle ages, see the preface to Raymond Klibansky (ed.), *Plato Latinus*, Vol. iv, *Timaeus A Calcidio Translatus Commentarioque Instructus*, J.H. Waszink (ed.) (Warburg Institute, London, 1962). Other partial sources for knowledge of the *Timaeus* in the middle ages were *The Consolation of Philosophy of Boethius* and Macrobius' exposition of Cicero's *Somnium Scipionis*. For information on the early sources of Greek science, see Marshall Clagett, *Greek Science in Antiquity* (New York, 1976), especially p. 185 ff. This study relies chiefly on the following works: William of Conches, *Glosae super Platonem*, *Texte Philosophique de Moyen Age*, Vol. xiii, avec introduction, notes et tables, E. Jeauneau (ed.) (Paris, 1965). Hugh of St Victor, *Didascalicon*, trans. Jerome Taylor (New York, 1968). Adelard of Bath, *Quaestiones naturales*, M. Müller (ed.), *Beiträge*, Bd. xxxi (Munich, 1934). Thierry of Chartres, *De sex dierum operibus*, N.M. Häring (ed.) (Toronto, 1971). Peter Abelard, *Theologica Christiana*, Migne, *Patrologia Latina*, CLXXVIII, 1123–1330.

17. R.W. Southern believes that these men did not, in fact, constitute a School of Chartres as Raymond Klibansky and others have long held. He does think that the men we are here concerned with were probably familiar with each other's work and consequently there is some value in considering them collectively. See his monograph *Platonism, Scholastic Method and the School of Chartres* (Reading, 1979).

18. See my article, 'The Heresy of Science: A Twelfth-Century Conceptual Revolution', *Isis*, vol. 68 (1977), pp. 347–62.

19. It is not inconceivable that these works were pondered over by Copernicus himself in the Renaissance. To illustrate this point, we might think for a moment of Francis Bacon, who, although he did not contribute to any substantive scientific work, was, in the eyes of the men who founded the Royal Society, the prophet of scientific methodology.

20. The use of the term *moderni* at this point is significant: it suggests a psychological readiness to dissociate one's thinking from the traditional wisdom of the *auctores*. For a discussion of this point, see my article 'Science, Reason and Faith in the Twelfth Century: The Cosmologists' Attack on Tradition', *Journal of European Studies*, vol. vi (1976), pp. 1–16.

21. For a lively account of this phenomenon, see Alexander Murray, *Reason and Society in the Middle Ages* (Oxford, 1978), especially Chapter 10.

22. On the literary uses of 'nature', see Ernst Robert Curtius, *European Literature and the Latin Middle Ages* (New York, 1953). Also see George D. Economou, *The Goddess Natura in Medieval Literature* (Cambridge, Mass., 1972). On the great question of why a particular era sees nature as it does, A.C. Crombie says, 'The commitments of a period to dominant general beliefs about nature and science make certain kinds of question appear cogent and gives certain explanations their power to

convince . . . because they establish . . . the kind of world supposed to be there to be discovered. It may be supposed to be a kind of divine economy . . . a system of mechanisms, or a manifestation of probabilities. Such beliefs establish the kind of explanation that will give satisfaction . . .' 'Historical Commitments of Biology', in *The British Journal for the History of Science*, vol. iii (1966) p. 98. The particular frame of reference used in the *Timaeus* made this work peculiarly appropriate to the cast of mind of the Western European in the early twelfth century.

23.   William of Conches, *De philosophia mundi*, PL 172, 3–102, IV, 32. There is a new edition by G. Maurach (Pretoria, 1980).

24.   Adelard of Bath, *De eodem et diverso*, H. Willner (ed.), *BGPM*, IV (Münster, 1904), p. 13, 1, 20.

25.   Robert of Melun, *Sententiae*, I, I, 28, Martin Gillet (ed.) (Louvain, 1952.)

26.   John of Salisbury, *Policraticus*, VII, 6, I.C.C. Webb (ed.) (Oxford, 1909).

27.   See *Glosae*, introduction, p. 24, fn. 1.

28.   For information on the extent and number of manuscripts of William's commentary, see Edouard Jeauneau (ed.), *Glosae super Platonem*. For information and elucidation on William's efforts to digest neoplatonic doctrine in his commentary on the *Timaeus* and also those he wrote on Macrobius, I refer the reader to fn. 9; see especially Tullio Gregory. For information on the extent of the medieval interest in the *Timaeus*, see Margaret Gibson, *Pensiamiento*, 25 (1969), pp. 183–94.

29.   *Prologus in Eptatheucon*, E. Jeaneau (ed.) in *Med. Stud.*, xvi (1954), p. 174.

30.   *Didasc.*, I.

31.   Ordo vero discende talis est ut, quia per eloquentiam omnis sit doctrina, prius instruatur in eloquentia. Cuius sunt tres partes, recte scribere, et recte pronuntiare scripta, quod confert *grammatica*; probare quod probandum est, quod docet *dialectica*; ornare verbe et sententias, quod tradit *rhetorica*. Initiandi ergo sumus in grammatica, deinde in dialectica, postea in rhetorica; quibus instructi, et ut armis muniti, ad studium philosophiae debemus accedere.' Cap X.L. I. *De philosophia mundi*, Libri Quatuor, p. 100, P.L. (under Honorius Augustodunensis).

32.   William's *Commentary on Macrobius*, Ms. Berne 266, fol. 3 va. William is concerned to accommodate Plato to Christian beliefs, e.g. his effort to suggest equating the *anima mundi* with the holy spirit, as do Peter Abelard and others. For details on this see Tullio Gregory, above, fn. 9.

33.   *Theol. christ.*, I, 5. For a thorough analysis of William's handling of the term '*integumentum*', see E. Jeauneau, 'L'usage de la notion d'"integumentum' à travers les gloses de Guillaume de Conches', in *Archives d'histoire doctrinale et litteraire du moyen age*, xxic (1957) pp. 35–100. William speaks contemptuously of those who are ignorant of the true significance of *integumenta*, and who cover up their ignorance with a moral excuse.

34.   *Commentary of Bernardus Silvestris on Martiànus Capella*, Cambridge University Library, Mm 1.18 ff. 1–28r.

35.   Garciones, garrulitati intenti, et nihil philosophia cognoscentes, et ideo significantiones ignorantes integumentorum, erubescentes dicere nescio, querentes solatium sue imperitie, aiunt hoc exponere trutannicum esse.' Quoted in E. Jeauneau, *Glosae super Platonem*, in *Textes Philosophiques de Moyen Age*, XIII (Paris, 1965), p. 51.

36.   'Quod satis Plato insinuat in suis libris per assumptionem in metaphorismorum, multa enim per lumen intellectuale vidit, quae sermone proprio nequivit experimere.' Dante, *Letter*, translation and notes by P. Toynbee, *Dantis Alagherii Epistolae* (Oxford, 1966).

37.   *Glos.*, p. 72. William of Conches was impressed by Plato's dictum that 'everything that exists necessarily does so owing to some cause, for nothing can come to exist without a cause.' (*Tim.*, 28A.) Peter Abelard cites this passage to prove that the cosmos is not governed by chance but by reason, in *Theologia christiana*, V, coll.

318A. John of Salisbury speaks of the *Timaeus* as a work 'which most subtly investigates causes in nature'. *Policraticus*, VII, 5.

38. G. Henderson, *Style and Civilization, Early Medieval* (Harmondsworth, 1972), p. 78.

39. *Didasc.*, II.

40. *Glosae*, p. 103.

41. *Glosae*, pp. 108, 109.

42. *Didasc.*, II.

43. On this subject see Gregory Vlastos, *Plato's Universe* (Seattle, 1975), p. 66 ff.

44. 'Sed creatio numerorum rerum est creatio.' *De sex dierum operibus*, xxxvi, 1. 46.

45. 'Plato enim, ut Pythagoricus, sciens maximam in numeris perfectionem . . . quippe cum nullatenus creatura sine numero possit existere. . . .' *Glosae*, p. 305.

46. G.E.R. Lloyd, *Early Greek Science: Thales to Aristotle* (London, 1970), p. 40.

47. And for the late twentieth-century readers it appears to be suggestive still. Efforts to synthesise the DNA molecule include a recent success in the synthesis of a molecular dodecahedron: '. . . the last of the five regular Platonic solids [as described in the *Timaeus*, 55 ff.] to be synthesized. . . . the high degree of symmetry of the Platonic molecules makes it possible to investigate the properties of chemical bonds in great detail.' *Scientific American* (January 1983), p. 72.

48. *Glosae*, p. 137.

49. *Dragmaticon*, 28D. For William's use of the term *elementum*, see T. Silverstein's 'Elementum: Its Appearance among the Twelfth-Century Cosmologists', *Med. Stud.*, xvi (1954), pp. 156–62. Also see H. Flatten, *Die Philosophie des Wilhelm von Conchos* (Koblenz, 1929), pp. 105–22.

50. *Glosae*, p. 252. Gregory Vlastos, after recapitulating the Greek beginnings of a theory of celestial motions, writes '. . . well before Plato's time . . . the role of observation had changed drastically in Greek astronomy since the days when rational inquiry into the heavens had begun in Miletus as a branch of *physiologia*.' He retraces the discovery of the planets and suggests that this was established before the *Republic* was written. Vlastos sees this discovery as evidence of a breakthrough in the area of empirical investigation and goes on to say that 'The creation story of the *Timaeus*, despite its allegorical tincture, attests Plato's assimilation of the results obtained by the [empirical] science in which theory and practice were now successfully interacting.' An analysis of Plato's demonstration of his grasp of contemporary astronomy in this dialogue follows. Vlastos, *Plato's Universe*, pp. 40 ff.

51. *Glosae*, 296, Appendix A.

52. *Glosae*, 252.

53. William writes, 'Dixerat primordiam materiam nullo nomine debere nominari propter mutabilitatem qualitatum circa ipsam. Hoc probat per simile, et hoc per ipothesim id est per positionem re quae nunquam visa est.' *Glosae*, 274.

54. *De eodem et diverso*, p. 13, Lines 19–21. See above, fn. 17.

55. On the subject of the element of uncertainty that is a necessary part of Plato's science, John of Salisbury writes that Plato's followers 'declare themselves uncertain, some about everything, some about everything which is not self-evident or incapable of being doubted.' *Meta.*, BK III (Oxford, 1929), 94 in the Webb edition.

56. He goes on to say that in the *Timaeus* 'the cause [*aitia*] of physical . . . phenomena are . . . derived synthetically from the structure of the atom. And what is claimed for them is not uncertainty, but verisimilitude, the atomic theory itself being presented as no more than a plausible hypothesis having no more than aesthetic elegance and the saving of the phenomena to recommend it.' G. Vlastos, 'Reason and Causes in the *Phaedo*', in *Plato: A Collection of Critical Essays*, Vlastos (ed.) (New York, 1971), vol. I, pp. 132–66. William of Conches writes that knowledge of *corpora*,

opinio, must necessarily be of a provisional nature, uncertain and subject to revision because it deals with material phenomena as opposed to the incorporeal, fixed truths available to men via the divine *intellectus. Glosae*, p. 281 ff. See Appendix, p. 5. The capacity to question and challenge conventional notions presupposes an awareness of the distinction between probability and certainty. G.E.R. Lloyd has an enlightening discussion on the Greek predilection for such original thinking in Socrates' day in *Magic, Reason and Experience: The Origin and Development of Greek Science* (Cambridge, 1979); see especially p. 252 ff.

57.   *Timaeus*, 27D, translated by Desmond Lee (Harmondsworth, 1977). Timaeus claims that his story is second to none in probability (also see 44cd, 48d, 67d). Vlastos's belief is that the *Timaeus* was especially designed for those for whom a purely Democritean materialism was unacceptable. 'For these [readers] the *Timaeus* offered a brilliant alternative. If you cannot expunge the supernatural, you can rationalize it . . . restricting its operation to a single primordial creative act which insures that the physical world would not be *chaos* but *cosmos* forever after. This Plato accomplished by vesting all supernatural power in a Creator who was informed by intelligence and was moved to create our world by his love and beauty and by his pure, unenvying goodness . . . He gave rational men a pious faith to live by in two millennia all through which science was more prophecy than reality.' (Vlastos, 'Reason and Causes in the *Phaedo*', p. 97).

58.   On the whole problem of the function and purpose of Plato's myth-making Gottschalk writes, 'For Plato, eschatology was an adjunct of ethics and the theory of knowledge. Vivid though his myths are, they tell us very little about the soul or its fate outside the body which is not directly relevant to its functions and duties while on earth.' H.B. Gottschalk, *Heraclides of Pontus* (Oxford, 1980). It is Plato's habit in his myths to convey a moral by giving an account of something '. . . about which he knows himself to be ignorant. We are expected to understand that the moral significance, so to speak, of the myth is to be taken seriously, but no more than that.' I.M. Crombie, *An Examination of Plato's Doctrine*, II (London, 1963), p. 199.

59.   *Timaeus*, 27A.

60.   See Richard C. Dales, 'Discussions of the Eternity of the World during the First Half of the Twelfth Century', in *Speculum*, vol. 57 (1982), pp. 502 ff.

61.   Brian Stock argues that the transition in this period from oral to written 'modes of communication was an important shaping instrument both for the forces of change and for the processes of thought by which they were simultaneously interpreted'. Brian Stock, *The Implications of Literacy: Written Languages and Models of Interpretation in the Eleventh and Twelfth Centuries* (Princeton, 1983), p. 531.

62.   *Glosae*, pp. 210, 211.

63.   *Glosae*, p. 254. Many scholars of our own day think that the *Timaeus* was written to form a continuum with the *Republic*. It was designed to appeal to the *physiologoi* — the *physici* of Athens who were intrigued by the new science of Anaxagorus and the other scientists — so as to entice them toward the widening of their perception of science and its uses. G.E.R. Lloyd points out, '. . . the spheres of law and justice provide models of cosmic order. The notion that the world-whole is a cosmos, that natural phenomena are regular and subject to orderly and determinate sequences of cause and effect, is expressed [in Plato's Greece] partly by means of images and analogies free from the legal and political domain.' (Lloyd, *Magic, Reason and Experience*, p. 247).

64.   A modern Plato scholar seems to think somewhat similarly: George Claghorn in *Aristotle's Criticisms of Plato's Timaeus* (The Hague, 1954), says 'Purpose is to be found in every individual thing and in the universe as a whole. [The *Timaeus* shows] man possesses his physical endowments in order to live the moral life (41d–42d, e) . . . Plato did not wish men to forsake science. He urged them to do all the research possible into earthly causes, but then to see the ultimate unity and rationality.

Science was not to be for its own sake, but for the welfare and betterment of mankind.'
(47b–3, 68e–69d), p. 128. Claghorn believes that Plato has never had his due in the
history of science: 'He has not only been misunderstood, but grossly underestimated',
p. 135.

65.   *Glosae*, p. 297.

66.   The frequent use of the analogy between the 'macrocosmos' — the universe —
and the 'microcosmos' — man — used by the poet Bernard Silvestris and other twelfth-
century writers comes via the *Timaeus*, although the metaphor itself is older; see, for
example, Bernard Silvestris, *The Cosmographia*, translated by W. Wetherbee (New
York, 1973).

2 The Role of Reason

Toward the end of the tenth century, Western Europe was sufficiently settled to bring a steady advance in political and economic strength. The growth in commerce and the concomitant development in the towns and cities brought with it the need for a literate class of laymen; at the same time, royal power had reached the point where a need for trained administrators was being increasingly felt. Hence, we see the appearance of a new type of educational institution, the cathedral school, in France and England, to supply society and kings with the necessary intellectual equipment to meet these new demands. These same prevailing economic and political conditions also fostered a new mood of optimism and confidence among those experiencing the benefits of this new security and prosperity. The intellectual and artistic revival of the twelfth century is a direct result of this mentality.

This new sense of self-confidence in men's ability to shape a future for themselves had the effect of releasing considerable sources of creative energy in Western Europe. By the twelfth century this innovative power had found expression in the technical efficiency of both Church and temporal government, in Gothic architecture, in the lyrics of the *vagantes* and Goliards, in the numerous glosses on Roman jurisprudence and in the vigorous interest shown in the new intellectual game of dialectic. Before the mid-eleventh century, men had experienced their world as lacking in order, unpredictable and hence largely unmanageable. For them, God and the whole range of divine forces alone had the power to impart coherence to human existence. R.W. Southern says:

> Man's links with the supernatural gave his life a framework of order and dignity; but in the natural order the chaos was almost complete. Almost nothing was known about secondary causes in natural events. Rational procedures in law, in government, in medicine, in argument, were scarcely understood or practised even in the most elementary way.[1]

But after the mid-eleventh century, men began to respect human abilities and potentialities, experiencing an impulse to invest man with new dignity and value, first as a means to a deeper understanding of God, and then as a means for greater understanding of man himself and the natural world he inhabits. The chaotic, unknowable nature of the universe is less often dwelt upon in the hymns and writings of the late eleventh century; and the new cathedral schools set themselves the task of extending 'the area of intelligibility and order in the world in a systematic way'.[2] The development of the *quaesio* at that time is a good example of this extension. From its origin in the tenth century as a means for codifying the growing body of canon law, it becomes a dialectical tool for the resolution of conflicting arguments and discordant opinions in patristic exegesis. The curriculum used at this time was the entire corpus of science as well as whatever techniques were available for utilising this knowledge.

By the beginning of the twelfth century, this programme of studies had so far progressed as to bring about a notable change toward the possibility of a sense of order in human experience. Men felt a greater sense of dignity than before as they came to see that by training the intellect they could add to the sum of knowledge and understanding of themselves and the world. As a consequence of this new sense of human dignity there was a recognition of the beauty and nobility of the created world. This aspect of twelfth-century humanism naturally followed, for if man sees himself as worthy of dignity then the natural order of which he is a part also participates in this sense of worth. An appreciation of the grandeur and beauty of nature becomes itself a human quality. Man takes his place in nature, and human society is seen as part of the grand complex of the natural order which is bound together by rational laws.

It began to appear that the whole universe was intelligible and accessible to human reason: nature is now perceived as an orderly system, not a mysterious, necessarily obscure phenomenon. And man, coming to a potential understanding of the laws of nature, can see himself as the main part, the keystone of the natural world. It is the possibility of such understanding that gave twelfth-century men the confidence in human powers, the confidence implicit in any humanist movement. 'When those elements of dignity, order, reason and intelligibility are prominent in human experience, we may reasonably describe as humanistic the outlook which ensues.'[3]

Implicit in this attitude toward mankind is the belief in man's capacity for learning, for development. The twelfth-century cosmologists, like humanists in other periods, hoped for some kind of human progress, and this hope found an outlet in the thirst for scientific knowledge evident in their works. The concept of progress has not often been associated with the twelfth century, but there is clear evidence that something very like it formed a component of the optimistic faith in *ratio* in this period.

It began to be apparent, then, that if a man could harness his reasoning faculty and train it to function well, he could with its help learn to understand the world. It was also clear to men at this time that this faculty was God's gift. John of Salisbury says:

> All who possess real insight agree that nature, the most loving mother and wise arranger of all that exists, elevated man by the privilege of reason, and distinguished him by the faculty of speech. ... While grace fructifies [human] nature, reason looks after the observation and examination of facts, probes the secret depths of nature and estimates all utility and worth . . .[4]

Such realisations brought fresh confidence and hope for increasing knowledge of nature and of man, and of the rewards such knowledge could bring. This new optimism was in part due to a sense that the past had been mastered and the future of knowledge about the universe was an open one — the first time this sense of intellectual potential and rational optimism had prevailed since the Greeks.

Bernard of Chartres expressed this mood when he wrote that the scholars of his age stood on the shoulders of the giant thinkers of the distant past, and therefore could see further than their predecessors. Thierry of Chartres, who died about 1150, inspired this epitaph:

> His eagle eye could clearly see
> Through each perplexed obscurity
> of all the seven liberal arts.
> He knew them well in all their parts,
> and made quite clear to everyone
> truth that for Plato dimly shone.[5]

The idea that Thierry could see further than Plato, not through revelation but through rational analysis was surely very bold.

The twelfth-century cosmologists had a firm faith in the progression of knowledge. They envisioned a chain of inquiry into and teaching of natural science, and they believed that the handing on of scientific study from teacher to student through the generations had a necessarily cumulative effect that would ensure the preservation of scientific knowledge and would provide for unlimited possibilities of advancement.[6] Such confidence was felt about man's ability to go forward in science that, for the first time since antiquity, the belief in contemporary ability to surpass the ancients was clearly and boldly expressed.

> In the twelfth century ... one of fiery and varied intellectual activity ... and independent thinkers who cannot be placed in any category ... there was a feeling of liberation, an exuberance over a dawning civilisation, an intellectual drive.[7]

The idea of a natural order, with its implied dependence upon the operation of a supreme, rational intelligence, revolutionised medieval thought. Such an orderly view not only altered radically the direction of theological thought in the twelfth century, but provided an incentive for independent scientific work. It also provided a rationale for confidence regarding the power of *ratio* to penetrate the obscurities of nature. Man, the possessor of a rational intellect — itself a link between the created universe and the divine world of the intelligence of God — man 'alone in the world of nature, could understand nature ... He alone could use the perfect nature in accordance with the will of God, and thus achieve his full nobility.'[8]

The ability to put what was known of Aristotle's logic to sustained and creative use engendered this belief in the power of the human intellect. Enough of the works on logic was known by the time of Erigena to affect his thought, but the full force of the intellectual revolution that the discovery of logic engendered began later.

> The generation that saw the death of John the Scot still regarded dialectic with good reason as a dangerous helpmate for theology. A hundred and fifty years later the logical analyses of Berengar evoked ... a notable storm, but the usefulness of his method was immediately acknowledged and imitated ... The knowledge of dialectic had developed under the aegis of several other branches of learning, and then it suddenly emerged into a brilliant pre-eminence.[9]

The popularity in the eleventh century of the writings of the so-called Hermes Trismegistus may have contributed to the new concern with man's rational facility. He divided the intellect into three parts: that concerned with seeking causes, that with *natura*, and that with reasoning processes.[10] It is certain, however, that the writings on logic which Boethius had assembled were already so thoroughly assimilated by the last quarter of the eleventh century, having been enthusiastically taught at the turn of the century by Gerbert, that the notion of applying dialectic to all kinds of knowledge began to be held by the dialectitions of the period. Dialectic had traditionally been defined, as Rabanus Maurus said in the ninth century, as 'a rational discipline of inquiring, defining, and discussing and also capable of discerning the true from the false'.[11] With Berengar of Tours (d.1088), this practice emerged as a conscious technique of rational thought.

> He is ready to state positively that reason and not authority, is mistress and judge. Dialectic is the art of arts, and it is the sign of an eminent mind that it turns in all things to dialectic. Anyone who does not do so abandons his principal glory, for it is by his reason that man resembles God. He intends, therefore, to have resort to dialectic in all things, because dialectic is the exercise of reason, and reason is incomparably superior to authority when it is a question of ascertaining the truth.[12]

Berengar's pioneering effort to subject Christian tenets to rational scrutiny were recognised, and opposed, by Lanfranc, who accused him of wanting to approach all problems through reason and forsake tradition. 'Reason arrives at truth by dialectic', says Berengar, 'which is superior to all authorities and which was used by Augustine and even by Christ himself. Whatever is illogical, notably, the doctrine of transubstantiation, is necessarily false'; and, '. . . Not by decrees of the Church . . . but by reason which is the image of God in man, do we alter the truth.'[13]

This passion for applying rational techniques to every kind of thought had a direct impact on science when Roscelin of Compiègne, a follower of the popular art of dialectic at the turn of the century, enunciated the nominalist theory which includes the idea that objects of our senses have a singular, individual identity or existence. He said that in nature the individual alone exists: '*Nam cum habeat eorum sententia nihil esse praeter individua.*'[14] Roscelin's position clearly implied the value of concrete, material sense-data, and this stimulated the scientist to accord greater importance to the practice of direct observation of the *res*, the phenomenon under consideration.

Anselm of Aosta's goal was 'to see with the eye of reason those things which in Scripture lay hidden in deep obscurity.'[15] He utilised rationalism in his theological speculations; his 'proofs' of God's existence are evidence of the power of this intellectual movement, for it is at this time that the habit of seeking proof for statements requiring belief was established. Reason, authority and experience were the three kinds of proof most commonly offered in this age, and of these reason was significantly favoured by Anselm in his orderly, logical presentation. Anselm held that the teachings of faith were ultimately rational, and he expressed a firm trust in the importance to the Christian of the functioning intellect. In *Cur deus homo* he wrote: 'It seems to me sheer negligence, being firm believers, not to be eager to comprehend fully what we believe.'[16] But, although Anselm's thinking was imbued with the rationalist temper, he himself reveals an anxiety about possible dangerous effects, as when he speaks of the *moderni* as heretics of dialectic who should be hissed away (*exsufflandi*) from discussions of spiritual matters.[17]

From Berengar on through Roscelin and Anselm, the new intense interest in *ratio*, in the application of the rules of dialectic, was focused with increasing sharpness upon problems related to Christian doctrine. Hence, it is the more remarkable that the cosmologists were, for the most part, able to leave this use of Aristotelian logic alone, and to invent instead a radically different use for the novel technique. It is precisely in this creative act that the importance of the cosmologists in the history of ideas lies. Hugh of St Victor suggests that there is a particular purpose to the rationality of the Creator's use of *ratio* in his structuring of the universe: '. . . in all things God proposed doing, he must have kept especially to that mode of action which best served the need and convenience of his rational creature.'[18] Hugh wrote that the nature of argument itself should be considered first:

Once this was known, then they [the ancients who perfected the technique of argumentation] could also know whether the results discovered by argument were truly held. Hence, skill in the discipline of true logic began — that discipline which provides ways of distinguishing between modes of argument and the trains of reasoning themselves, so that it can be known which trains of reasoning are sometimes true, sometimes false, and which never false . . . It is logic which ought to be read first by those beginning the study of philosophy, for it teaches the nature of words and concepts, without both of which no treatise of philosophy can be explained rationally . . .[19]

The cosmologists reasoned, in effect, thus: God has given us His gift of the capacity to reason. When we develop this divine gift, we can use it productively and, in doing so, enhance what is most distinctively human in us. The created universe operates according to basically rational principles, having been deliberately so designed by its Creator. Man, by virtue of his capacity for reasoning, and because he is part of a rational cosmos, is fitted to understand the ways in which the natural world functions. The cosmologists arrived at this conclusion, which implied the need for a new discipline, natural science, by means of a perfect Aristotelian syllogism. Eduard Jeauneau points out that there is a basic agreement in approach between William of Conches and Thierry of Chartres regarding the role of reason in creation. While recognising God's primacy in the act of creation, nevertheless both emphasise everywhere a rigorously rational explication, or, as Thierry insists, 'Only according to physical laws — according to *natura*, according to *rationem physicorum*.'[20]

Although twelfth-century men were cognisant of the kinds of objections being made to the practice of scientific inquiry, the first task that they approached was to imbue their contemporaries with their own trust in a rational nature. In his commentary on Genesis, Thierry of Chartres explained that the created world is so constructed as to exhibit in the highest degree a rational and beautiful order, as it was created by God alone. Thierry believed that this beauty and order (*rationabiliter*) exist as a consequence of being in accordance with the wisdom of its Creator. When Adelard of Bath opposed the common opinion that the fact that grass exists can be explained only as 'a wonderful effect of the wonderful Divine Will', he said that of course it was the Creator's will that grass exists, 'but it is also not without a natural reason' and he reiterates, 'But there is nothing [in nature] without *ratio*.'[21] William of Conches makes the same point with more heat:

> But I know they will say that although we are in fact ignorant of how God did this [i.e. transform a tree into a calf] we know that he can. Pitiful wretches! What is more pitiable than such a statement? For whatever God is able to do he does not necessarily do; and to argue that he can cause something to occur in nature — something that is neither visible, nor is according to reason nor is useful in any way — does not prove that he will do so.[22]

The cosmologists' credo is pronounced by William: 'The world is an ordered aggregation of created things.'[23] Honorius of Autun speaks of the lawful regularity of the universe:

> The entire fabric of the world — consistent, though made of such dissimilar parts [is] one, though composed of such diverse things; tranquil, though containing such opposed elements — continues in its lawful and ordered way: solid, harmonious and with no dread prospect of ruin.[24]

Honorius includes in his version of the theme the idea of a harmonious whole, an idea that fostered an appreciation of the aesthetic appeal of nature. Elsewhere he talks of '. . . creation coming to fulfilment in a universe in which natures of diverse character insure an overall harmony; it is in the integration existing among these that the greatness of God's plan lies.'[25] Hugh of St Victor wrote with certainty of the rational principle underlying the universe:

> The ordered disposition of things from top to bottom in the network of this universe . . . is so arranged that, among all the things that exist [in nature] nothing is unconnected or separable by nature, or external.[26]

Thierry of Chartres said, 'The world would seem to have causes for its existence, and also to have come into existence in a predictable sequence in time. This existence and this order can be shown to be rational.'[27]

Adelard of Bath is persuasive on this point:

> For truly, whoever abolishes [in his mind] the innate order within nature is mad. Therefore to establish chaos as its base (and origin) is arguing necessarily from foolishness. For He who disposes is most wise. Consequently, He least of all is either willing or even able to abolish the fundamental order in nature . . . and among philosophers it is agreed that any upsetting of this order is least likely to occur.[28]

When questioned about the nature of the stars, Adelard replied, 'For whatever is in or on these [stars], I consider that they are the product of a rational nature.'[29] Seizing on a biblical reference (Wisdom 2:21) to drive this point home, he writes elsewhere:

... whence it happens that the visible universe is subject to quantification and measure and is so by necessity. For each thing exists [in nature] either as one or as many. The immense universe itself is also defined by the fact of its being limited by its very nature.[30]

Measurability defines the universe by means of a terminal boundary, and the universe is hence finite. The emphasis is on the knowability of nature by its property of being limited, which in turn has two implications: it can be understood because it has its limits; and, because quantification and measure are properties of all natural phenomena, mathematics is an important tool for attaining knowledge of nature. The use of the adjective 'immense' reflects the confidence Adelard feels in his scientific enterprise, as if he were saying that the cosmos may seem dauntingly large, but that it is, in fact, open to human comprehension by its very constitution, and thus there is no need to feel helpless before it.

Adelard goes back to the *Timaeus* for his argument:

The best author of created things, drawing all things to a likeness of himself, as much as their nature allows, equipped soul [*anima*], which the Greeks call *nous*, with understanding. In just this way nature is, then, like its Creator, purposeful, logical and free from chaotic confusion. This soul comprehends nature in itself — its causes and first principles ... and is also able to discover the theory behind these things.[31]

By implication, man too can dig out these causal laws and come to understand their operation. With calm certainty Adelard of Bath encourages a fellow scientist:

Nothing is difficult unless you despair ... therefore hope and you will discover a solution to the [scientific] problem. For I feel quite able to shed light on this matter, since we must assume that all of nature is based on a sure and logical foundation ...[32]

For Adelard, this thesis is no longer a position to be argued — it has become a self-evident proposition.

Adelard of Bath often expressed his belief in man's innate capacity for rational thought. At one point he presents an almost Darwinian argument:

Although man is not armed by nature nor is naturally swiftest in flight, yet he has that which is better by far and worth more — that is, reason. For by the possession of this function he exceeds the beasts to such a degree that he subdues them ... You see, therefore, how much the gift of reason surpasses mere physical equipment.[33]

At another, he echoes Aristotle: 'Man is a rational animal and for that reason he is sociable as well; and he is innately fitted thereby for the two operations of deliberation and action.'[34] Adelard thought that man's rational faculty helped him to deal with his emotions: 'Reason was a necessary function of the soul as an aid for moderating or controlling the passions, and was not lacking from it.'[35] In another place he says, 'In war, anger provides the motivation; in peace, reason does the pacifying.'[36] William of Conches saw the reasoning mechanism as underlying all mental functions:

These are the different powers of the mind: intelligence, reason and memory. Intelligence is that force of the intellect whereby man perceives the immaterial, after reason has made him certain of the cause of its existence. Reason — that force or function by which the mind is able to compare and contrast that which exists with other existent things. Memory is that function which allows man firmly to retain what he has thus previously understood.[37]

According to Southern, the cosmologists saw that:

... man's affinity with every part of nature gives him the power to understand everything in nature; that his elements and humours ... are the raw materials for the whole universe. Hence man, being the epitome of the universe, is built to understand the universe.[38]

Since nature is seen as amenable to predictability in terms of cause and effect, it was clearly akin to human rationality.

It is not easy for the twentieth century to apprehend the force of this revolution in thought. Instead of being a formless, incomprehensible magma, subject to obscure, arbitrary forces and supernatural powers the cosmos came to seem a coherent, harmonious unity, governed by laws. The universe and humanity had intrinsic qualities, a validity of their own.

Honorius of Autun goes on to develop the idea of man as an intrinsic part of nature:

Whence came the corporeal substance used in man's creation? From the four elements, and for this reason man is called a microcosm — that is, a lesser world; for from the earth he has his flesh, from water his blood, from air his breath and from fire his warmth.[39]

Thierry of Chartres expresses the same idea at the close of his commentary on Genesis, when he says that his book has unity and that this unity is a correlative of the unity of creation. (Just such a consciously constructed unity is seen in Dante's *Commedia*, in which the poet's function is performed in accordance with the root meaning of the word 'poet': πόητης — one who makes or creates.)

That man is a part of a rationally planned and executed universe was a liberating notion for the twelfth-century writers. It is not surprising that, with the freshly perceived relevance of this idea to the new sensitivity to nature at this time, the concept of a reified nature — the hypostasising of the natural world as 'Natura' — was also vigorously revived. The twelfth century was familiar with this classical conception. Ovid uses it in the *Metamorphoses* (I, 5 ff.); he begins his cosmogony by a description of chaos and mentions 'a god or milder nature' bringing an end to the conflict that is Chaos. Claudian also wrote of Natura as a cosmic power. In Lucretius, Venus is the creator of universal life, and she governs the nature of things; Lucretius also refers to her as *'natura creatix'* (*De rerum nat.* I, 21 and II, 1116). Martinus Capella speaks of Natura as *'generationum omnium mater'* (*Marriage of Philology and Mercury*). This universal goddess was not merely the personification of an intellectual concept, but was one of 'the last religious experiences of the late pagan world'.[40]

Natura appears frequently in many kinds of writings during this period: in John of Salisbury's work[41] and in Bernard Sylvestris' curious poem *De mundi universitate* (*cosmographia*), the goddess Natura plays a central role, much of which is of pagan provenance. This centrality, combined with the evidence of the work's interest for its contemporary readers, reflects the importance of the concept of nature in this period.[42]

Adelard of Bath attempts to reconcile the doctrine of God's all-compassing power with a belief and trust in a rational universe:

I do not detract from the power of God, for all that exists does so from him and by means of His power. However, this is not to say that nature itself is chaotic, irrational, or made up of discrete elements. Therefore it is possible for men to achieve an understanding of this rational order inherent in nature, an understanding as complete as the extent that human knowledge [*scientia*] progresses ... Consequently, since we do not turn pale before our present state of ignorance about nature, let us return then, to the method of reason.[43]

God's ultimate power does not imply its random or arbitrary use, and the fundamental rationality that pervades every part and aspect of the cosmos also means that everything in it somehow fits — that there is an overall harmony and balance. This statement is remarkable for its confidence in science, and in its imaginative grasp of the possibility of continuing development. The concept of progress, which is probably a *sine qua non* for all sustained effort in science, is here articulated. The reference to 'our present state of ignorance' is evidence of this certainty of the bright future of the new endeavour, the discipline of natural science.

The very notion of progress, so common a thought to twentieth-century minds, is here a radical notion deserving of at least passing treatment, inasmuch as it represented an articulated programme of improvement of the condition of man with the ensuing implications of an optimistic mood, a sense of confidence and an increasing control over both environment and experience, novel predicates in the twelfth century to a novel idea.[44] The men here treated called themselves the *moderni*. As was the more famous case of the Renaissance, there was here a moment of discontinuity during which they broke away from their past in a conscious and purposive manner.

They had a heady sense of possibility, a sense that they could, through knowledge and investigation, improve the lot of humanity and, through an increase in the pool of human knowledge, alter the course of man's development, for the better. This is all the more remarkable considered against the prevailing view of history at this time, when all metaphors of time focused around Augustine's notion of the totality of history leading only toward the Heavenly City.

Guy Beaujouan warns us not to overemphasise the rationalist impulse of the twelfth century. He mentions that Thierry's biblical commentary does not claim to be compelling as proofs but rather as, in his own words, 'intellectual steps toward consolidating the Faith'.[45] I cannot agree, however, that the impulse to set forth *probationes* expressed by Anselm, Thierry of Chartres and the other cosmologists was a response to any perceptible weakening of the Christian faith in this period. I see it purely as a powerful need to harness the intellect in the service of all experience, including religion.

Indeed, the *moderni* reinvented science. Science is an attitude toward experience consisting of a systematic application of mental effort toward gaining more knowledge and applying it, once gained, to actual life. The Augustinan view of progress as a movement during time toward a condition of betterment hung upon one weak peg: that this betterment was a paradise to come only after this life ends. But the *moderni* had a vision of an earthly progression in time in which they could participate through rational effort directed to scientific exploration and expansion of knowledge.

To sum up, the steps whereby the cosmologists constructed a dialectical bridge from God, the ultimate source of reason, to the pursuit of science, are as follows: since God is supremely rational, men might properly assume that His creation (i.e. all of nature) obeys logical principles. It follows that man, participating in the divine gift of a rational faculty, has the ability to penetrate the mysteries that nature presents to him. And it necessarily follows that man is not only equipped to do this, but that it is his clear duty to do so. For such work helps to celebrate the glory of God, exercises man's highest function and is of use to his fellow men. Such was the impulse and such the frame of mind that helped to focus attention on scientific inquiry.

Notes

1.   R.W. Southern, *Medieval Humanism and Other Studies* (New York, 1970), p. 32. The outburst of creative energy in the twelfth century was free enough to allow for the revival of such literary forms as satire, a form which requires of the writer a degree of detachment from the social scene. Raby notes that 'The appearance of satire usually implies a society which has reached a high state of development, a civilization of towns, and considerable freedom of thought. These conditions were fulfilled in twelfth-century France, and this explains the reappearance of poetical satire.' F.J.E. Raby, *A History of Secular Latin Poetry in the Middle Ages*, 2nd ed., Vol. II (Oxford, 1967), p. 287. We will examine another aspect of this quality of intellectual critical detachment in Chapter 4.

2.   Southern, p. 37. Andrew of St Victor (*c*. 1140) wrote 'Ab otiosis et in tempore otii et non a discurrentibus et perturbationis tempore sapientia discitur.' Quoted in Beryl Smalley, *The Study of the Bible in the Middle Ages* (Oxford, 1952), p. 356.

3.   Southern, pp. 31–2.

4.   *Metalogicon: A Twelfth-Century Defense of the Verbal and Logical Arts of the Trivium*, I, trans. Daniel D. McGarry (Berkeley, 1955), p. 9.

5.   A. Vernet, 'Une Epitaphe inédite de Thierry de Chartres', *Recueil de travaux offert à C. Brunel*, ii (1948), pp. 660–70. (Quoted in part.)

6.   Edgar Zilsel, 'The Genesis of the Concept of Scientific Progress', in *Roots of Scientific Thought*, Philip P. Wiener and Aaron Noland (eds) (New York, 1960),

p. 252. He writes, '. . . the ideal of scientific progress includes (1) the insight that scientific knowledge is brought about step by step through contributions of generations of explorers building upon and gradually amending the findings of the predecessors; (2) the belief that this process is never completed; (3) the conviction that contribution to this development, either for its own sake or for the public benefit, constitutes the very aim of the true scientist.' Zilsel believes that this concept was first articulated in the beginning of the fifteenth century.

7.   Emile Bréhier, *Histoire de la philosophie: L'antiquité et le moyen age*, III, trans. Wade Baskin as *The Middle Ages and the Renaissance* (Chicago, 1967), p. 59.

8.   Southern, p. 50.

9.   R.R. Bolgar, *The Classical Heritage* (New York, 1964), p. 154.

10.   'Tria sunt que intellectum hominis perfectius formant, componunt et constituit. Causa scilicet, ratio et natura. Causa suum causatium precedit. Ratio componentem intellectum et dividentem efficit. Natura unicuique rei non solum esse sed etiam tale esse constituit. Ratio ex causa et ex utraque natura. Causa est inter prima principium substantie non vocis ratione suum precedens effectum. Ratio est vis quedam a causa procedens cuncta a principio ordinans . . . Hic igitur tria, causa scilicet, ratio et natura, prius intellectum formant ad cognitionis aptitudinem . . .' Pseudo-Hermes Trismegistos, *De VI Principiis*, cap. 1; ms. Bdl. Digby 67, f69r-v.

11.   *De clericorum institutione libri tres*, PL 107, col. 397.

12.   Berengarius, *De sacra coena*, as quoted in David Knowles, *The Evolution of Medieval Thought* (New York, 1964), p. 95.

13.   *De sacra coena*. See Stock's discussion of Berengar, *Implications*, p. 279 ff.

14.   Roscellinus, '*De generibus et speciebus*', in *Ouvrages inédits d'Abelard*, V. Cousin (ed.), p. 524. See also Andrew of St Victor: 'Verumtamen in scripturarum expositione cum secundum naturam res de qua agitur nullatenus fieri potest tunc demum ad miracula confugienda noverit.' From the *Commentary on Ezekiel*, quoted in B. Smalley, *The Study of the Bible in the Middle Ages*, p. 145. John of Salisbury uses this idea in his explanation of Gilbert de la Porrée's science, 'Utebatur, prout res exigebat, omnium adminiculo disciplinarum, in singulis quippe sciens auxiliis mutuis universa constare.' *Historia Pontificales* xii.

15.   Eadmer, *Vita Anselmi*, trans. R.W. Southern (*The Life of St. Anselm*, Oxford, 1962, p. 12).

16.   *Cur deus homo*, c.2.

17.   *De fide trinitatis*, pp. 158–9.

18.   Hugh of St Victor, *De sacramentis*, as quoted by Chenu, p. 18.

19.   *Didascalicon*, trans. Jerome Taylor (New York, 1961), p. 59.

20.   Quoted from *Hexaemeron*, in *Note sur l'école de Chartres*, p. 4.

21.   *Quaes.*, p. 6. 'Sed eadem sine ratione non est.'

22.   *Phil.*, III. 'Sed scio quid dicent: Nos nescimus qualiter hoc sit, scimus Deum posse facere. Miseri! Quid miserius quam dicere istud, est? quia Deus illud facere potest, nec videre sic esse, nec rationem habere quare sic sit, nec utilitatem ostendere ad quam hoc sit. Non enim quidquid potest Deus facere, hoc facit. Ut autem verbis rustici utar, potest Deus facere de trunco vitulum: fecitne unquam? Vel igitur ostendant rationem, vel utilitatem ad quam hoc sit, vel sic esse indicare desinant.'

23.   *Glossa in Timaeum*, p. 125. 'Et est mundus ordinata collectio creaturarum.'

24.   *Elucid.* (PL CLXXII 1116), translated in Chenu, *Nature, Man and Society*, p. 26. '. . . nec tota illa mundi fabrica sine ulla ruinae formidine ex tam dissimilibus partibus uniformis, ex tam diversis una, ex tam contrariis quieta, et solida et concors in sua lege perseverat et ordine.'

25.   *Sacramentis*, as quoted in Chenu, p. 5. The sense of wholeness of nature that is here expressed was a part of the new awareness of nature and we are not surprised to find that the word *universitas* was first used in this period as an independent noun. Father Chenu says that it first appeared in a work by Geroch of Reichersberg.

De Aedificio Dei, in which Geroch writes, '... totam universitatis structura convenienter ornatur.'

26. *Sacramentis*, i2.2 (PL CLXXVI 206). 'Rerum omnium ordo dispositioque a summo usque ad imum, in universitatis huius compage ita ... prosequitur, ut omnium quae sunt, nihil inconnexum aut separabile natura externumque inveniatur.'

27. *De operibus*, p. 172. 'Causas ex quibus habeat mundus existere et temporum ordinem in quibus idem mundus conditus et ordinatus est rationabiliter ostendit ...'

28. *Quaes.*, p. 66. 'Qui vero rerum ordinem tollit, insipiens est. Ab insipiente igitur hanc confusionem constitui necesse est. Rerum vero dispositor sapientissimus est. Minime igitur rerum ordinem tollere vel vult vel potest, quare nec hanc transpositionem stare possibile est. In philosophantis itaque animum id incidere minime conveniens est.'

29. *Quaes.*, p. 63. 'Quidquid enim in ipsis vel ab ipsis fit, ratione provida fieri aestimo.'

30. *Eodem*, p. 23. 'Unde fit, ut universa visibilia numero subiecta sint, et huic etiam cadem subici necesse sit. Quicquid enim est, aut unum aut plura est. Ipsam illam etiam immensam universitatem termini limite definit sibi certo atque naturae.'

31. *Eodem*, pp. 9–10. 'Rerum conditor optimus omnia ad sui similitudinem trahens, quantum eorum natura patitur, animam mente, quam Graeci noyn uocant, exornauit. Hac ipsa, dum in sua puritate est, tumultu exteriore carens plane utitur. Nec modo res ipsas, verum etiam earum causas et causarum initia assequitur et ex praesentibus futura longo tractu cognoscit; quidque ipsa sit, quid mens, qua cognoscit, quid ratio, qua inquirit, deprehendit.'

32. *Quaes.*, p. 58. 'Nihil est difficile, nisi cum desperes. Spera igitur et facultatem invenies. Ego quantum potero, rem delucidabo. A constanti itaque et indubitato principium sumendum est.'

33. *Quaestiones naturales*, p. 20. 'Tamen nec arma sibi innasci convenit nec levissima fuga aptari. Habet enim id, quod his longe melius digniusque est, rationem dico, qua etenim adeo ipsa bruta excellit, ut per eandem domentur ... Vides igitur, rationis donum corporeis instrumentis quantum praecella.'

34. *Quaes.*, p. 20. 'Homo quidem animal rationale atque ideo sociale est, aptum ad duas operationes, actionem dico et consilium, quod aliis appellare placet bellum et pacem.'

35. *De eodem et diverso*, pp. 15–16. 'Sed et ipsae eius potentiae, ira, dico, et concupiscentia, a sua moderatione quandoque aut declinaturae aut casurae erant, utpote a corporeis passionibus irritandae. Ratio igitur huic ad has revocandas et necessaria erat et ab ea non aberat.'

36. *Quaes.*, p. 21. 'Quippe quorum unum (i.e. bellum) ira movet, alterum (pacem) ratio mitigat.'

37. *De philosophia mundi*, 'Hujus animae diversae sunt potentiae, scilicet: *Intelligentia, ratio, memoria*, et est *Intelligentia* vis animae, qua percipit homo incorporalia, cum certa ratione quare ita sit. *Ratio* est vis animae, qua percipit homo quid sit, in quo conveniant cum aliis, in quo differant. *Memoria* vero est vis, qua firme retinet homo ante cognita.'

38. Southern, *Medieval Humanism*, p. 40.

39. Honorius of Autun, *Elucidarium*, as quoted by Chenu, p. 29.

40. Ernst Robert Curtius, *European Literature and the Latin Middle Ages*, trans. W. Trask (New York, 1953), p. 107.

41. John of Salisbury, *Entheticus*, Webb (ed.), pp. 258, 625.

42. Peter Dronke, 'Bernard Silvestris, Natura and Personification', *Journal of the Warburg and Courtauld Institutes*, vol. 43 (1980), pp. 16–31.

43. *Quaes.*, p. 8. 'Deo non detraho. Quidquid enim est, ab ipso et per ipsum est. Id ipsum tamen confuse et absque discretione non est, quae, quantum scientia humana procedit, audienda est. In quo vero universaliter deficit, ad Deum res referenda est. Nos

itaque, quoniam nondum inscitia pallemus, ad rationem redeamus.'

44. For a discussion of the medieval attitude to progress, see A.C. Crombie, 'Some Attitudes to Scientific Progress, Ancient, Medieval, and Early Modern', *History of Science*, 13, (1975), pp. 213–30.

45. Guy Beaujouan, 'The Transformation of the Quadrivium', in *Renaissance and Renewal in the Twelfth Century* (Cambridge, Mass., 1982), p. 482.

3 The New Conception of Science

Having conceived and formulated the idea of a serious, concerted enterprise — the sustained search for knowledge of nature — a conscious impulse was transformed into a genuine programme for science, to be drawn up, delineated, taught, promoted and defended. Before we examine this programme, we might note the growth of interest by some Western Europeans in the scientific activity in the adjacent Islamic and Byzantine areas.

In the last quarter of the eleventh century, a marked acceleration in the exchange and translation of scientific works of Greek and Arabic provenance took place in southern Italy and Spain. Of the men trained in these scientific worlds, we know of two who wrote percipiently on scientific problems in the West. One of these was Pedro Alfonso, a Spanish Jew who settled in England around 1110 and later was employed as physician to Henry I. Alfonso wrote that scientific knowledge was important and ought to be widely studied, and to that end he recommended the substitution of medicine for the traditional study of grammar, a suggestion of revolutionary boldness at a time when the liberal arts curriculum had been frozen by many centuries of tradition. Another startling pronouncement of his was his insistence that the scientist be ready to apply personal experience, direct observation, to the subject under study; his own profession of physician most probably made him particularly aware of the importance of the empirical method for science. Alfonso explained that the scientist who neglects this method is rather like a goat who, missing the ripe fruit, is limited to green leaves for his diet. Persuasively appealing to students on behalf of the scientist's discipline, he said that:

> As far as I am concerned, I have no interest in giving vent to my views to people who already know, nor am I concerned to dismiss anything before proof has been provided; for the concepts of science should first be grasped through experience. In the same way, no man can be recognized as a teacher of science without [citing] proof.[1]

Walcher of Malverne was another knowing writer on science, a French monk who wrote on astronomy *c*. 1090. Walcher has left an account of an eclipse of the moon — a rare example of original, individual scientific observation during a period when such personal initiative was strikingly absent, and, moreover, one which was singularly free from the expressions of awe or fear that characterised observations of such natural events in the eleventh century.

Although men such as Alfonso and Walcher were certainly rare in this period, it becomes possible to discern the appearance of a separate group who felt themselves to be distinctive because of their interest in intellectual matters. The spread of the cathedral schools situated in the flourishing towns added to the number of educated men. Men trained in these schools in the twelfth century (*scholastici*) were quite different in their interests and ambitions from those educated in the monastic schools (*claustrali*). The *scholastici* included students from the merchant class as well as from the aristocracy, and many hoped to qualify for the new government posts then being created by the innovative courts of the English and French monarchies. The new schools were far more lay-oriented than were the monastic schools, for the latter were chiefly concerned with educating priests. The *scholastici* became a kind of intellectual élite and were increasingly aware of their difference from other, less literate people; within their own ranks they began to generate an intellectual climate that was freer and more congenial to those who were attracted to science.

In this bracing climate, the new *scholastici* viewed themselves as *moderni*, and as strong partisans of the new as against the venerated past. The *saeculum modernum* was consciously felt to be qualitatively distinct not only from the distant past but also from the comparatively recent past, and the scholars of the early twelfth century saw their age as far more significant than merely the turn of a century: indeed, they felt themselves to be on the threshold of a new and different age. From the first appearance of *magister* as a professional title in the schools, *modernus* was attached to it to distinguish the medieval teachers from the ancient authorities.[2] The first collection of statements by the modern men to be presented parallel with the pronouncements of the ancients was made in the first decade of the twelfth century by Manegold of Lautenbach. This new impulse to champion the present surely attests to the vigour of the rationalist movement, and the strong sense of general security and economic well-being that was experienced in the intellectual centres of the West.

Contrary to the impression given by many medieval historians that the *scholastici* were chiefly occupied with theological problems, there was in fact much activity concerning speculative and practical science.[3] Some *scholastici* began to refer to themselves as *physici*, the old term for physician, but used now in the sense of one concerned with the systematic investigation of *physis*, nature. This is a telling piece of evidence of the birth of a new discipline, illustrating the sense of common purpose felt by these adventurous spirits and their determination to gain knowledge and understanding of the hitherto inscrutable mind of nature.

This small band of intrepid scientific pioneers worked out a programme for themselves, their students and prospective colleagues, which included formulating convincing reasons for embarking upon scientific study. For the ancient Greeks an innate propensity for questioning everything was enough; for medieval men, more was necessary. The twelfth-century scientists saw the importance of explaining their motives for engaging in the new work; but this required that they themselves formulate the reasons clearly. William of Conches, in an emotional passage on rhetorical problems, gives vivid expression to what is probably the deepest motivation for the scientist in all ages — the need to get at the truth; for as Mount Everest is climbed 'because it is there', so must the scientist, when presented with a natural mystery, try to find the solution to it.

> Anyone who finds himself put off by the dryness of our discourse, would be much less apt to miss rhetorical embellishments if he fully understood our intention; for if he did understand he would more likely be astonished at how much we have accomplished. . . . But although many demand a display of rhetorical skill from writers, we know of few who require truth from them. Few even recognise it when they see it, and none of the common people [*multitudine*] do; but of those few who actually boast of their honesty, we alone, in fact, sweat out the truth [*soli veritati insubabimus*]. And we prefer to present that truth in a naked state rather than clothed in lies.[4]

The passionate sincerity and indignation shown here attest to the genuineness of William's commitment to science and also to the validity of his personal experience of it. His defensiveness on the subject of his writing suggests that these cosmologists were being criticised for a new style of scientific writing. There is a curious parallel between William of Conches's efforts to evolve a writing style which, in its clarity, precision and directness, would be especially suited to the expression of scientific thought, and efforts made in the same direction by seventeenth-century Englishmen who were organising a scientific programme.[5] William's reputation as a great teacher of rhetoric made him particularly vulnerable to criticism; his irritation with the obtuseness of his critics in the passage quoted above suggests real opposition to his work and ideas.

Besides the spur of intellectual curiosity, William gives another reason for engaging in science: he thinks that the active search for scientific knowledge is a truly Christian endeavour. In such work he believes that the scientist is not only acting in accordance with Christian tenets, but the more vigorously a rational course is pursued in this direction, the better Christian one becomes. Hence the scientist is exhorted to try every means towards this end before accepting literal Scriptural explanations for natural phenomena — this is itself a motive for science. William says that though it might be necessary to rely upon scriptural explanations, one ought to postpone doing so. When the individual student of science feels that he has exhausted his own capacities in his rational search, his next step should be to seek out colleagues so as to pool all possible human intellectual resources. This step, unfortunately, is rarely taken.[6]

His appeal for a communal, concerted effort in scientific research comes a century before Roger Bacon's famous proposals. He sees clearly the need for more than individual work if science is to yield maximum results. When one considers the very short interval in the medieval period in which consciously scientific work had been carried on when William was writing, he appears remarkably perspicacious in thus foreseeing the proper direction his discipline should take. The note of sarcasm at the end of the paragraph suggests again resentment at the behaviour of many hostile colleagues. Reiterating his position on the religious value of science, William says elsewhere '. . . by the knowledge of the creature we attain knowledge of the Creator'.[7]

Adelard of Bath suggests another motive for engaging in scientific inquiry when he quotes Virgil: 'Happy is he who can understand the causes of things.'[8] This quotation from the most beloved of Roman poets reminds us how steeped in classical literature the men of the early twelfth century were. Adelard is not proselytising here; he is merely echoing Virgil and the whole Graeco-Roman attitude towards the acquisition of knowledge. It is probable, too, that he knew Cicero's version, that among the activities most important to man are 'the contemplation and the study of the heavenly bodies and of those secrets and mysteries of nature which reason has the capacity to penetrate' (*De finibus*, V, 21, 58).

Adelard believed that rational man ought to be putting his divine gift of reason to use and also that in studying nature he was proving his right and exercising his privilege in being a part of it.

> You say that if anyone living in a house is ignorant of what it is made, of its size and quality and layout, he is unworthy of its shelter; and that, just so, if anyone born and educated in the residence of this world neglects learning the plan underlying its marvellous beauty, upon attaining the age of discretion, he is unworthy and, were it possible, deserves to be cast out of it.[9]

There is a degree of overstatement here that reveals Adelard's enthusiasm for science; neither William of Conches nor Thierry of Chartres ever goes this far in crying up the scientist's craft. Adelard's awareness of the aesthetic appeal of nature finds support here.

Elsewhere, Adelard shows his deep certainty of the essential rightness and aesthetic fitness of everything in nature. When queried about the comeliness of a face disfigured by the effects of a head cold, he replied, 'There is nothing in nature either dirty or unsightly. But, whatever is contrary to the *ratio* of nature, however much is added to the handsomeness of a face [e.g.] by painting it, we have the right to call dirty and ugly.'[10] His dislike of artifice, together with his strong championing of the rightness of nature, is here rather like Rousseau's. There is no attempt to idealise nature, but only a desire to hold up for admiration the natural world, the cosmos, an orderly functioning entity, pleasing to the eye and to the imagination. Another expression of wonder at the beauty of the universe as a work of great skill is by a coeval of the cosmologists, the monk known as Pseudo-Hugh of St Victor; he writes of '. . . the beauty of the universe, the intricate contrivance of heaven and earth, this marvellous and delightful work . . .'[11] There is in all these exclamations a sense of the complicated and elaborately interconnected nature of this creation; the cosmologists experienced its enormous complexity and beauty as twin aspects. Bernard Silvestris's great poem *Cosmographia* has many allusions to the harmonious beauty of the universe.

The new conception of the rationality of the universe that the twelfth century absorbed from the *Timaeus* brought with it a feeling of awe and admiration for a system so beautifully designed. The cosmologists rejoiced in this feeling, and were thereby released from the attitude of *contemptus mundi*. Their experience was channelled into religious expression: for the first time since antiquity — and more than a century before Roger Bacon articulated the thought — these writers made explicit the idea that the ultimate purpose of examining and investigating the created world was not primarily for the acquisition of scientific knowledge for its own sake, but was to help men to reach a higher level of understanding of the Creator.[12] William of Conches emphasises this in his commentary on the *Timaeus*.

Richard of St Victor thought that the celebration of the *ornatus* of the created world was a necessary stage for Victorines in their ascent to an understanding of God.[13] Honorius of Autun wrote, 'All of God's creation gives great delight to anyone looking at it, for in some things there is beauty, as in flowers; in others healing, as in herbs; in others food, as in produce; in others meaning, as in snakes [and birds].'[14] One finds references often to utility in science; awareness of practical usefulness and a degree of mastery over nature came with the advent of Arab science, particularly medicine, in the West.

To sum up, the twelfth-century scientists (or cosmologists) urged the scientific investigation of the natural world as a duty of a Christian, undertaken in gratitude for the magnificent gift of the cosmos, as a suitable response of rational man, aware of his kinship with nature and with his God in terms of his rational capacity; as a source of pleasure and happiness, as a means of celebrating the glory of God's work, and as a source of mastery and use of nature for the benefit of man.

Although we use the term programme for the working-out of the pursuit of natural science as a separate branch of study, it should not be inferred that the twelfth-century men who were concerned with this matter were organised or systematic in their exposition of their programme. For though the cardinal points of a viable approach to science as a discipline were well understood, the necessity for systematising was not seen then; and so we are compelled to impose a kind of order on what was, for the most part, random and unconnected, dispersed throughout these men's works. Even if the cosmologists did not consciously set about framing a scientific programme, they did have a coherent plan of procedure which justifies our use of the word programme. This programme included a community of *physici* who worked co-operatively to solve scientific problems.

The value of communal efforts for the practice of science was well understood. If the cosmologists could not predict the teamwork of the modern laboratory, they at least saw the importance of sharing their investigations and approaching scientific problems in the company of their colleagues. Mutual discussion and reflection were most helpful to the inquiring scientist. Adelard compliments his nephew's exposition of a thorny question, 'Thus reason advances and we think alike.'[15] In a discussion with a colleague on the importance of logically-based theories in natural science he says, 'Continue, therefore, between you and me, reason only shall be judge . . . since you are proceeding according to the rational method I will give reason and take it, too.'[16] And again, he encourages his colleague, '. . . and since the first question has been solved by reason, if you have doubts about others, speak up.'[7] Mutual discussion of theories and hypotheses helps to correct errors, curbs a too inventive imagination and pools the intellectual resources of the group, while encouraging bold, independent thinking.

Adelard has thought this method through in answering a question about the function of hair on the human body:

> Since these matters that have to do with the visible, as I judge matters concerning the evidence of the senses themselves to be capable of being explained, let us begin to discuss these matters. For there is nothing in the physical make-up of a human being that is, in my judgment, too difficult to be either understood or eventually solved through mutual reflection and discussion — and rightly so. For while the unlettered either question the truth of natural science and ascribe it to false writings fraudulently added to reliable authorities, or judge such knowledge to be essentially without value — these people, when they try to discover something about nature for themselves fail, because they are unable to carry on a [rational] discussion. As Boethius says in his work on music, 'among philosophers it is possible to entertain doubts or uncertainty concerning sense data, whereas this state of mind is unknown to the ordinary man'. Therefore, let us learn by examining what you have believed to be accepted knowledge on this point.[18]

Adelard makes a basic distinction between the trained thinker and the untrained: only the former can carry on an objective discussion of an abstract problem. Only the trained thinker has the capacity to remain for a time in a condition of uncertainty — able to reject, at least temporarily, that comfortable certainty with which the human mind is most at ease when evidence is not in accord with currently accepted explanations, or when evidence falls outside a preconceived framework and thus requires a degree of daring to interpret or apply to reality. The ability to reserve decision requires considerable courage, Adelard is saying, and is the more difficult in that it often means going against a traditional opinion on the question involved.

In short, the twelfth-century men who wrote on approaches to science, stressed the need for co-operation among those engaged in scientific research and inquiry. The need for pooling resources was well understood, and also the value of patient work and slow reflection on problems, always keeping the provisional and tentative nature of the hypothesis being formulated well in mind.

William of Conches broke ground in attempting to define science by fixing a point of division within the realm of philosophy between metaphysics and science. 'Up to this point', he says, 'we have limited our discussion to those categories which include the existent and the not visible, and now we will turn our study to those things which are existent and visible.'[19] The reasoning processes of the *physici* are of a different order from those of the metaphysician and theologian, who are concerned with problems about essences and substances not visible to the human eye. Struggling to discriminate between the province of natural science and the province of metaphysics, William writes:

> Those particles which you say are elements, are they visible or not? If they are visible they do not lack the quality of divisibility [i.e. they are not capable of being reduced to component parts], if they cannot be seen, since they can be perceived by no other sense, then this can be understood in the way Lucretius describes: from things inaccessible to the senses do not believe that information about sense-data can be deduced.[20]

Later in the century, Garnerius of Rochefort tried to clarify this point:

> For in mathematics one examines the visible forms of visible things; in physics, the invisible causes of visible things; in symbolism one juxtaposes and adapts visible forms to demonstrate invisible things; in theology one contemplates invisible substances and the invisible natures of invisible substances.[21]

The business of defining and classifying the sciences was a necessary step taken at this period.

Before natural science could be given an accepted place in the curriculum of the schools, before it could properly be advocated, supported, promoted or taught, it was necessary to know precisely what it was. In the *Didascalicon de studio legendi* (also known as *Eruditionis didascalica*), a treatise on the liberal arts written by Hugh of St Victor around 1140, Hugh examines the arts and divides science into four classes: theory, practice, mechanics and logic. He saw the sciences as having been first developed as a set of customary usages in response to human needs, and later reduced to formal rules. By 'mechanics' he meant the providing of those things that are necessary because of human frailty, and he included navigation, agriculture and medicine among them.

In Thierry of Chartres's manual on the arts, *Heptateuchon*, written in the same period as the *Didascalicon*, practical science is emphasised: geometry, arithmetic and works dealing with surveying and measurement, practical astronomy (dealing with calculations for calendar purposes) and medicine, all are prominent in this handbook of studies. In the majority of textbooks in Paris at the end of the century, as, indeed, in the writings of Albertus Magnus and Roger Bacon in the following century, a particular stress on technology or practical science is to be found. However, such emphasis seems not to have taken over in the curricula of the new universities, where science was, for the most part, taught as a theoretical discipline, except, of course, in medical schools such as Salerno.[22]

Thierry believes the *trivium* equips the philosopher for the study of material science. In the prologue to his handbook, Thierry advocates the trivium as indispensable for a command of language, and the *quadrivium* for the study of nature. Holding a comprehensive view of the scope of philosophy, he writes with enthusiasm: 'We have coupled the *trivium* and the *quadrivium* as partners in a marriage so as to propagate a noble race of philosophers.'[23]

The *De divisione philosophiae* of Dominicus Gundissalinus (Gundisalvo), written *c*. 1150, is usually considered the most important classificatory work on science in the twelfth century. Utilising the Arabic tradition of classification, Gundisalvo classes the sciences as either theoretical or applied — '*Una consistit in sola cognicione mentis, altera in execucione operis.*' The theoretical sciences were physics, mathematics, theology. He speaks of physics as:

providing knowledge of natural bodies through observation of their sensible aspects, and proof from their intelligible aspects . . . The instrument of this art is the dialectical syllogism, which is based on what is true and probable. . . The practitioner is the natural philosopher who, proceeding rationally from the causes of things to the effects, or from effects to causes, seeks out principles.[24]

We will return to this lucid definition of the function of deductive reasoning in science.

Gundisalvo divided the *artes* into two groups: the propaedeutic disciplines, or *scientiae eloquentiae*, which included logic as well as grammar, and the philosophical disciplines, or *scientiae sapientiae*. He thought that '*nulla est scientia quae philosophiae sit aliqua pars*'. The practical studies included *ethica*, *economica* (comprised of *artes mechanicae* and *politica*), *perspectiva* (optics), *de ponderibus* (weights) and *de ingeniis* (machines, or mathematical devices). Actually, each of these sciences consisted of a theoretical part which studied basic principles and a practical part, in which these principles were put to use. Arithmetic in an applied form included the abacus used in commerce. Gundisalvo adds for each science its 'definition, genus, material, species, utility, aim, instrument, who uses it, its etymology and in what order it should be studied'.[25]

William of Conches draws up a schema of the sciences in the prologue to his commentary on the *Timaeus*. His primary division is into preparation for eloquence and preliminary work for gaining knowledge. The former comprise the trivium, and the latter are divided into *practica*: ethics, economics and physics (the study of nature). The quadrivium is a subheading under mathematics, and within the four sciences are many subdivisions. The importance assigned to mathematics in the early twelfth century was greater than it had been in previous medieval centuries, and greater than it was in subsequent centuries until it was again subject to renewed interest in the sixteenth century.

Historians often assert that, as Southern says, 'The necessity for a thorough study of the secular sciences as an introduction to theology became one of the basic principles of medieval theological teaching . . .'[26] In the light of Thierry's remarks quoted above on the value of the quadrivium in his popular curriculum pamphlet, this assertion needs some qualification. For the chief purpose of the study of the quadrivium in Thierry's and William's eyes was to advance the study of natural science. Why this motive was afterwards overlooked by the universities is a question that bears further investigation. It is still not clear why the promising beginnings made in science in our period did not develop into a full-fledged scientific movement until four more centuries had passed.

It is clear then, that the efforts of twelfth-century scholars to clarify the natural sciences methodically as a prerequisite guide for teaching them led to important results in the ways in which science was to be thought of and approached. For one thing, the handbooks we have considered were widely read in Western Europe and, for this reason, helped to widen and promote the appeal of the discipline. The focus on technological sciences was a departure in attitude from previous times, and this emphasis on the useful sciences led to the articulation of a new aim or goal for the study of science: to control nature for man's benefit and use. Finally, the intelligent effort to define (more precisely) and classify the sciences led to a new refinement and awareness of approaches and methodology in scientific study. The handbooks of the early twelfth century did much to augment the work of the translators in the dissemination of awareness of, and informed interest in, natural and applied science.

Thierry of Chartres's handbook on the liberal arts, the *Heptateuchon*, has been called 'the best monument we have of the complete arts course before it was drowned in the flood of new material and new interests in the late twelfth century'.[27] Thierry's view of the basic importance of the quadrivium is echoed in the manner of the depiction of the sciences on a portal of the cathedral of Chartres, which was under construction during Thierry's chancellorship. It is believed that this sculpture is the first representation of the seven liberal arts to be made on a façade of a cathedral. This work on the Royal Portal of the cathedral symbolises the rational works of man and is a part of an elaborate, well-planned iconographical work.

In Thierry's handbook, he specifically connects the quadrivium with the need for increased understanding of God. He uses the mathematical symbol of the square to illustrate by rational means both the creation by the Father of the Son and the idea of the equality of the Son with the Father:

The place accorded the Liberal Arts at Chartres has special significance. Decorating the archivolts, they were brought into a direct relation to Jesus enthroned. The instruments of human wisdom exemplified at the periphery of the tympanium are thus bound to Divine Wisdom in the center. This makes it clear that man's striving for knowledge is dependent on and directed towards Divine Wisdom.[28]

Other church façades built in the second half of the twelfth century also included the secular studies of the schools in their iconographical scheme — for instance, 'Natural Science' is personified on the north portal of Notre Dame in Déols. In illuminated Scriptures of the mid-twelfth century, 'philosophy' is personified rather than 'wisdom'. Philosophy here signifies the seven arts. An example is the Bible from St Thierry at Rheims, which shows a female figure, Philosophy, holding forms which contain figures representing respectively Natural Science and Logic.

From the time of Roscelin of Compiègne, the philosophical problem of universals gained wide attention. In the first half of the twelfth century the terminology of the dispute became common coin among intellectuals. Roscelin's position concerning the importance of the individual *res* did not have a direct influence on the development of science until it was amplified and explored by Occam in the fourteenth century, but it had an indirect influence and it did contribute to twelfth-century scientific thought. Now let us see how the individual sciences were perceived.

Adelard of Bath attempts to define astronomy:

> For astronomy is that discipline which deals with the shape of the world, the measuring of its circumference, the route or path of the planets; it also describes the structure of the constellations, depicting their position and colour.[29]

Adelard's reference to the zodiac, although seemingly demonstrating an area of fuzziness in his idea of the boundary between astronomy and astrology, should not be taken as a definite sign of unscientific thought, since he may be referring to the zodiac simply in the sense that it formed a convenient map of the heavens, and one familiar to most of his fellows; this area remains murky, to some degree, well into the sixteenth century. William of Conches also tries, and with more success, to clarify this problem:

> There are three modes of treating those matters that are outside the range of our vision — fable, astrology and astronomy. The first tells of the origin of the heavenly signs, such as Taurus the bull, the second treats of what is said to appear in the heavens, whether they

exist or not, and the last, astronomy, deals with the problem of the existence of those things said to be in the heavens — whether they are visible or not.[39]

The four basic sciences — arithmetic, geometry, music and astronomy — are seen by Thierry of Chartres as of the greatest importance in the training of the scientist. If we want fully and deeply to comprehend the craft and art of the Creator, we must train ourselves in those disciplines — mathematical proofs, music, geometry and astronomy — as the workings of created nature reveal themselves by these approaches and are shown to be perfectly rational. In Thierry's thought, arithmetic and geometry are especially required for an understanding of nature, since God has arranged that all existent things have both qualitative and quantitative aspects.[31] Again, Thierry argues:

> there exist four kinds of rational disciplines which lead men to an understanding of God as Creator — namely, the proofs [demonstrations] of arithmetic, music, geometry and astronomy. As tools for theology, these disciplines are to be used sparingly, so that the craft of the Creator may appear in the [natural] things themselves; and that which we propose may be rationally shown.[32]

In the early twelfth century, logicians were the first to grasp the idea of a theoretical scientific explanation. These men, using only the portion of Aristotle's logic transmitted by Boethius (known later as the *logica vetus* and revived as a study in the tenth century by Gerbert) recognised, as Crombie says, 'the distinction between experiential knowledge of a fact and rational or theoretical knowledge of the cause of the fact, by which they meant knowledge of some prior principles from which they could deduce and so explain the fact.'[33]

According to E.J. Dyksterhuis, the ideal methodology for scientific study includes the forming of inductive hypotheses based on careful observation of the phenomena; mensuration and the mathematical formulation of results (which, in turn, allow for prediction that can be verified quantitatively); and the deductive framing of a set of concepts which illustrate the functioning of the investigated phenomena. The twelfth-century scientists, although they could not formulate this ideal methodology, did understand it. They made some mistakes, however, and one of them, Dyksterhuis believes, was to overestimate the value of mathematics for physics. This is an understandable mistake to make in an age which had no devices to assist the eye in observation; Greek science had been handicapped in the same way.[34] However, it will not do to accuse the cosmologists of neglecting empirical methods, as we will show later. Dyksterhuis's methodology puts deductive reasoning last in the formulation of scientific hypotheses, but for the cosmologists it also came first; for finding the cause of a natural problem meant also to apply Plato's 'give the reason', to use logic to attack the problem initially. 'Give the reason' could mean deductive theorising in search of causal principles.

William and the other twelfth-century scientists often pose the problem of the use of some natural phenomena, referring to the idea that everything in nature serves some function in terms of the whole. William writes:

> The peasants say God can make a bull calf from a tree. We say: but has he ever done so? Therefore those who make such statements must show the reason or the use of his doing such acts, or they had better desist from making these assertions.[35]

Frequent reference is made to the *rustici* by William and others of his group, always in the sense of ignorant and superstitious men. The purpose seems to be to shame the reader or student into thinking harder; possibly this tactic is the more successful because many students have come from the peasant class. (Some, of course, did come from the noble class, as did Abelard.) The derisory use of *rusticus* is evidence of a new sense of community among the educated men in the towns.

The deductive theorising for causal laws was seen as a necessary but extremely difficult task. Adelard of Bath writes:

> For the functioning and interconnection between all the senses are manifest in all living things, as Boethius attests. But which forces come into play in what connections, with which method or mode, none except the mind of a philosopher can make clear and evident. For the effects of these interactions are most subtly connected with their causes and [sometimes it happens that] the relationship between the causes themselves is also very subtle, that often knowledge of these matters is concealed from philosophers by nature itself.[36]

This passage shows an intuitive grasp of the biological process: Adelard grasps the complexity of interchange and interaction in organic life. He sees the difficulty the scientist often has in separating cause and effect; when he speaks of nature as deliberately hiding her methods of operation from the investigator, he does it with optimism — as a challenge which the scientist can meet.

The chief approaches to science were understood by the early twelfth-century scholars. The empirical and logical were both seen as necessary; inductive and experimental techniques were necessarily joined to mathematical–deductive reasoning.[37]

In the *Didascalicon*, Hugh of St Victor writes:

> The proper function of mathematics is to deal clearly by means of reason with confused, actually existent things ... For instance, in the actuality of things no line exists apart from surface and solidity ... but reason considers the line purely *per se* without surface or thickness. And this belongs to mathematics not because it is or can be so in things, but because reason often considers the acts of things not as they are, but as they can be, not in themselves, but as they might appear to reason itself ... logic and mathematics are prior in the order of learning to physics, and in a certain manner, function for it like tools about which anyone must first learn before he gives his attention to the study of physics. [*Ergo*] it is necessary that these sciences put their consideration not in the actual state of things, where experience is deceitful, but in reason alone where there is firm truth; and then with reason as the guide they could descend to experience of things ... Physics [*physica*] investigates the causes of things in their effects and the effects from their causes ... Physics thus tries to isolate the principles behind the appearances of things.[38]

Hugh saw clearly the reciprocal relationship between logic, mathematics and the scientific method.

Peter Abelard sets forth the function of deductive reasoning in scientific investigation as follows:

> Some sciences are concerned with action, others with understanding; that is, some consist in constructing things, others in analysing compound things. For many people are practised in action but have little scientific understanding; they have tested the healing power of medicines and are good at healing because of their

experience alone, but they do not know much about the natural causes . . . The man of understanding is he who has the ability to grasp and ponder the hidden causes of things. By hidden causes we mean those from which things originate, and these are to be investigated more by reason than by sensory experiences . . .[39]

Using the *logica vetus*, probably Galen and other writers — including Arabic works on medicine translated by Constantinus Africanus — Abelard shows his clear perception of the difference between empirical knowledge of a fact and rational understanding of the reason for the fact. Although Abelard concentrated on the deductive side of science, he 'was so far empirical as to hold that to know is to affirm as existing together what exists together in reality, the universal being a *nominum significatio* signifying the coexistence, so that the event is the cause of the truth of the proposition.'[40] Abelard's preference for the deductive aspect of knowledge was typical of the deep respect for every type of mathematical thinking felt in the twelfth century; there was an element of certainty about it that was very satisfying.

Plato's emphasis on the connection between natural science and mathematics strongly influenced the early cosmologists, and so, too, did his bias in favour of this type of knowledge. For empirical knowledge seemed to him only provisional, lacking in absolute reliability; whereas mathematically-based evidence or explanations had a basis of precision, and systematic steps that could be verified, 'proved', and hence trusted by the inquiring scientist. Such a view reinforced the reasoning procedures being learned with enthusiasm in the early twelfth century from the *logica vetus*, so that it became increasingly difficult to resist the seductiveness of mathematical reasoning. The pursuit, then, of purely rational explanations for natural phenomena became almost a passion in this period. The mathematical method was often called the scientific method, and new attention was paid to the importance of learning arithmetic, geometry (and music) as a propaedeutic to the study of astronomy, medicine, physics and other branches of science that could be strictly demonstrated from mathematical principles.

The medieval scientists were probably aware of Augustine's interest in the concept of mensuration in science. Gerbert (*De libero arbitris* II, XI-XVI) made a real contribution to the development of mathematics. Although he died at the beginning of the eleventh century, he exercised a seminal influence on the cosmologists through his pupil Fulbert, who as the founder of the school at Chartres, was able to inject into the curriculum a strong bias in favour of mathematics and science. The cosmologists had great confidence in the power of mathematical methods to yield scientific knowledge. We have already quoted Adelard of Bath discussing the idea that 'the visible universe is subject to quantification and measure'. Elsewhere he says:

> For the Greeks thought of geometry as a measuring of the earth. This discipline is of necessity by virtue of its usefulness to men, and it is easy to conclude that whoever understands the *ratio* of the earth will perceive this.[41]

There is a demonstrable continuity in Pythagorean theory from Pythagorus himself through Plato, who in the *Timaeus* conceived of 'substance as mathematical form which gave order to the disorderly movements of chaos' (*Timaeus* 27C). Number and extension formed the being of things and caused the world to develop by the penetration of number into the primal matter. Primordial matter was seen by Adelard of Bath as indestructible: 'And in my judgment nothing in this world of sense ever perishes utterly, or is less today than what it was when it was created. If any part is dissolved from one union, it does not perish but is joined to some other group.'[42] Basic elements are composed of this primordial substance, and such elements are, says William of Conches, *simplae et minimae particulae*, in which the four traditional elements which we see are established.

The twelfth-century scientists followed this mathematical line of thinking, as did those who followed them all the way into the seventeenth century. The Greek geometrical method was eventually transformed into a basic scientific tool of modern science. If, as Crombie believes, Robert Grosseteste was the first to explore this method systematically as a basic structure of scientific methodology, Adelard of Bath and others, living a century before Grosseteste, clearly and frequently expressed their belief in its importance. These men had learned from the *Timaeus*:

> ... the conviction that the basis of any satisfactory physical science must be sought in mathematics, and in the sense of provisionality of all results attained in physical science, and the consequent necessity of systematical and accurately registered experimentation if we are to be duly acquainted with the

'appearances' to be 'saved' by scientific theory.[43]

We must keep in mind, too, that the cosmologists were writing before Euclid's work was readily available in the West. The reluctance to 'descend', as Hugh St Victor puts it, from the area of truths that logic and mathematical reasoning gives to 'experience of things' is often rationalised.

The cosmologists' bias in favour of mathematics as a prime technique for scientific inquiry had its concomitant bias against relying on the evidence of the senses. Adelard says that the senses are reliable neither in respect of the greatest nor the smallest objects: 'Who has ever comprehended the space of the sky with the sense of sight? . . . Who has ever distinguished minute atoms with the eye?'[44] Adelard, probably thinking of astronomy, feels acutely the short-comings of man's sense equipment and sees the need for a determined effort to counteract the human desire to rely upon the senses for gathering scientific data. 'For knowledge [*scientia*] is of value when it derives not from sense-impressions but from ideas. It is for this reason that my friend Plato calls the senses irrational.'[45] Adelard deplores man's frustrating limitations: 'Oh the perversity, the ambivalence of things! When nothing is more reliable than reason, nothing more deceiving than the senses!'[46]

Thierry of Chartres feels no such frustration. In a passage explaining the passage in Genesis about God separating the waters, he rationalises by showing that clouds are in reality masses of water-vapour which are caused by the condensation of the heated water on the earth's surface. He says:

It is the nature of heat to divide water into minute drops and it appears that those tiny drops, by virtue of their nature, rise up in the air like smoke from a furnace. And so also it is seen in the heavenly clouds.[47]

Thierry offers as proof the observable fact that when you take a hot bath, the amount of water lost in the bathtub is present in the room as water vapour.[48]

The importance of experience 'was clearly seen in the early twelfth century'.[49] For the apprentice scientists of that period were deeply impressed by the medical empiricism displayed in so many Arab treatises, and they came to appreciate the need to get at the empirical facts first. They came to see that:

the only 'criteria of truth' were logical coherence and experimental verification. The metaphysical question about why things happen ... gradually gave place to the scientific question about how they happen, which was answered simply by a correlation of the facts by any means, logical or mathematical, that was convenient.[50]

In this period there was a passion for technology, for the practical effort that required manual skill and technical knowledge; such an interest resulted in the framing of questions in such a way as to encourage the experimental, the hypothetical. Even where no actual experiments were performed, a theoretical empiricism showed itself in a long tradition of 'thought experiments'.[51]

The familiarity felt in the twelfth century with the practice and theory of experiment and the usefulness of empirical evidence is shown in technological advances such as the invention of the water-wheel for processing cloth, the watermill, the windmill and the remarkable series of structural devices incorporated in the new cathedrals being built at that time. Such advances illustrate a prevailing concern for seeking practical solutions with experimental efforts, such a concern led to a new care for precision and exact measurement.[52] By far the most popular translations of Greek and Arabic treatises were those of a distinctly practical nature: instructions on the way to calculate and measure to get a more accurate calendar, practical manuals on chemistry (such as the *Mappae Clavicula*, an edition of which was produced by Adelard of Bath), various kinds of compass charts, and works on the use of the abacus, the astrolabe and other instruments.

A great influence on twelfth-century writers on science was a concept of Galen, who postulated a distinction between empirical and rational knowledge which he described as the *via experimenti* and the *via rationis*. Empirical evidence was sought in the former, and the latter proceeded by deduction from current theory, which in turn was the result of experience; Galen believed that in medicine it was most fruitful to combine both methods.[53]

Twelfth-century scientists used Euclidian terminology to designate the two aspects of scientific methodology: *resolutio* (ἀναλύσις) signified the movement from experience to theory, effect to cause, differentiated particular to unified universal; *compositio* (σμνθέσις) from theory to experience, and so on. These terms are used by Chalcidius in his widely-read commentary on the *Timaeus*: he states that to carry out philosophical research properly, it is necessary to combine the methods of *resolutio* and *compositio*. Erigena was familiar with this terminology and used it in his *De divisione naturae*; the double movement or process was the basis of his entire structure of thought.

The lively interest in technology is shown in the cosmologists' choice of examples and metaphors as well as in the literal meaning of their writing. William of Conches considers nature's method of operation:

> The work of nature is to bring forth like things from like through seeds or offshoots, for nature is an energy inherent in things and making like from like. The work of an artisan is a work that man engages in because of a need, as making clothes for protection against cold or a house against bad weather.[54]

Here William refers to the practical skills, revealing the consciously analytical concern for utilitarian interests of his age — the first period in Western Europe to appreciate the importance of technology.

> But in all that he does, the artisan imitates nature, for when he makes clothes he fashions them after the natural disposition of the body's members; and when he makes a house he remembers that water that collects on flat surfaces makes wood rot, whereas it flows down off slopes and cleans them, so he makes his roof peaked.[55]

This portion reflects the empirical element in William's science; reading it we feel the influence on William of the architects who were actively engaged in the pragmatic solving of construction problems at, perhaps, the cathedral at Chartres. The passage shows that in a period when substantial technological advances were being made, the men writing on science kept the lessons of close observation well in mind. And conversely, the artisans and craftsmen who applied science took advantage of the new work in science. An example is the use to which masons, who were involved in every aspect of designing and building new cathedrals, put mathematics.

> Medieval man was far more interested in pattern than we are. Geometry is the obvious example ... They had a passion for seeing circles and squares in everything and in transforming natural organic forms into those shapes that would confirm the

patterns their minds sought. Their search for God was in one aspect a search for order. Geometry could express this order more convincingly for them than any other medium except music.[56]

The rise of technology accompanying the rationalist movement was remarkable. Not only were the brilliant solutions found that led to the construction of Gothic church buildings, but many others which were to have a great effect on the economy. All these utilitarian devices were based upon, and corroborated, the ultimate predictability and lawfulness of nature experimentally ascertained and systematic- ally verified. Such uses to which a knowledge of nature was being put at this time suggested the possibility of mastery in nature, an idea that probably originated in Islam. (The ancient Greeks did not use it.) For the Arabic treatises now being translated stressed the concept of making nature serve man, of gaining power and control over it.

The cosmologists used inductive reasoning and were aware of the role of probability in formulating scientific hypotheses. We have already seen how William of Conches connects the realm of the visible with probability. The cosmologists were quite free of the medieval compulsion to demand certainty in their assumptions; Adelard uses the capacity to remain in a state of uncertainty as a touchstone for the trained mind.

John of Salisbury reflects the cosmologists' views on the relation of probability to problems in the natural sciences. The task of natural science is not an easy one; and in this it is less certain than mathematics. It can observe only the ordinary course of events, from which it determines the probable, the more probable and the necessary; and dialectic, inquiring into truth, makes use of the instrument of moderate probability (see *Meta.* II, 11, 427B). Nevertheless, the physicist would be guilty of overconfidence in his own strength if he should think he could arrive at a sure knowledge of all possible and necessary eventualities contained in the powers of nature (see *Meta.* II, 13, 870D), the roots of which are in the will of God.[57]

Adelard himself is careful in his inductive processes; he is anxious to take into account every fact available about the phenomena on which he is basing a hypothesis: 'Indeed, what you think of as least plausible in this matter [my explanation] actually saves the basic order and reason of natural processes.'[58] He courageously offers the less rather than the more plausible theory. This is evidence of Adelard's respect for nature's complexity and the difficulties attendant upon efforts to elucidate it. 'Save appearances' meant account for the total phenomena; this was a formula that goes back to Simplicius, a sixth-century commentator on Aristotle.[59] Following Aristotle's dictum that nature does nothing in vain, it was felt that the business of the scientist was to construct theories and hypotheses which kept this idea in mind.

Adelard of Bath, trained (as he says) by Arab scientists, keeps the phenomenon always in mind. Although, as indicated above, he was fully alive to the paradoxical element in sense-data he was vehement in his scorn of those who would deliberately discount their value for the scientist. He explains that the five senses are the servants of the seven arts, and without them these studies are powerless to produce knowledge. The senses are priceless jewels, but philosophers cannot simply put them to use as aids to knowledge. Instead they have divided themselves into two camps: one sees the senses as the source of all knowledge, the other, of all obscurity and deception.

> For to one [faction] knowledge necessarily derives from sense-data, for the other, it arises out of things unavailable to the senses; one proves that much of it comes from our senses; another intuits that knowledge is beyond the reach of the senses . . . They hold that nothing in the senses is certain — neither eyes or ears are to be trusted . . . Let those men be struck blind and deaf![60]

To sum up, the empirical-inductive, the theoretical-deductive and the purely mathematical were three approaches to the study of natural science in the early twelfth century. In the following century Robert Grosseteste and Roger Bacon set forth a systematic scientific methodology using these approaches. Not only did the twelfth-century writers anticipate many aspects of later thinking on this matter, but there is evidence that Adelard of Bath, William of Conches and the other men we have mentioned were known to these thirteenth-century scientists. It seems fair, therefore, to say that the debt of the later men to the efforts to the men of the twelfth century has not yet been sufficiently acknowledged.[61]

As we have seen, the cosmologists recommended that scientists engage in rational discussion. A prime purpose of such discussion was the fostering of a spirit of disinterest and unemotional attention to the particular aspect of nature under examination. The leap of imagination required to conceive of the separate, distinct discipline of science includes an idea, an ideal if you will, of objectivity — the ability (much rarer than we might think) to eliminate the self, and objectively to assess the evidence collected from sense impressions and mathematical measuring, from logical inference and inductive hypothesising. In fact, the concept of objectivity is, in a sense, the very concept of science. And with this attitude consciously maintained, the cosmologists perceived the possibility of conducting a rational search for natural causation. In this they were following Plato, who in the *Timaeus* constantly urged those investigating natural phenomena to 'give the reason' (λόγον διδόναι), and repeatedly stressed the dictum 'whatever comes to be must be brought into existence by the action of some cause'.[62]

Strict objectivity and detachment were not congenial to the medieval mind, and it seemed necessary to exhort those engaged in the search for knowledge of nature to practise an unemotional, deliberative attitude. Peter Abelard says that he who would achieve *scientia* is he 'who is able to deliberate upon and comprehend the hidden causes of things.'[63] The aspect of provisionality was perceived as necessary to the inquirer. The rationalists stressed a probing and analytical frame of mind in scientific matters, an attitude memorably encapsulated in Abelard's dictum 'By doubting we come to inquiry, by inquiring we perceive the truth.'[64] This emphasises the creative effect of such systematic doubt. The early twelfth-century cosmologists felt a strong impulse to look askance at experience, to criticise, to analyse objectively, to subject their world to a fresh, individual scrutiny quite independent of current or past beliefs. Adelard tried to awaken his fellows to the use of such a critical attitude — so much more bracing and enterprising, he believed, than a passive state of admiration for the unknown:

Why are you so completely absorbed in your admiration [of nature], why do you persist in marvelling — in your wonderment? Why do you constantly fluctuate between trusting in the *ratio* of nature and feeling a deep mistrust of it that reveals itself in your expression? And yet I fully understand the stubborn need to hold on to a kind of dark and determined ignorance concerning nature, for such a need is universally felt by a majority of men — they feel that they must doubt the existence of order and regularity in nature ... Therefore, unless you prefer not to know, approach the [scientific] problem directly. For everything that I have found out [about nature] has been by this plan. That is why I undertake any such problem with this procedure, and those who will neither accept this method nor heed my explanations — they point the finger at me and impute to me madness.[65]

If we reflect how often we remind ourselves today to abjure our subjective leanings, we will be better able to imagine the difficulties involved in gaining acceptance of Peter Abelard's message in the twelfth century: of all the new scientific ideas introduced to medieval Europe in this period, that of methodical doubt as a technique for the would-be scientist was probably the most difficult — and the most strange.

Notes

1. The 'Disciplina clericalis' of Petrus Alfonsi, trans. E. Herries and P.R. Quarrie (eds) (London, 1977), p. 70.
2. Chenu, *Nature*, p. 319.
3. Richard Lemay writes, 'Dispassionate examination of the rich manuscript materials remaining from this period has resulted in nothing less than a rediscovery of some major aspects of twelfth-century intellectual life. Whether in astrology or alchemy, in medicine or mathematics, in geometry, botany or minerology and et cetera, the intellectual pursuits of twelfth-century scholars appear to have ranged well beyond the pale of religious thought . . .'. *Abu-Ma'shar and Latin Aristotelianism in the Twelfth Century* (Beirut, 1962), p. xxv.
4. *Phil., Praef.* 'Si quis tamen est cui ariditas nostri sermonis displiceat, si nostri animi occupationes cognoverit, non tantum ornatum sermonis non quaeserit, sed de illo quod agimus stupebit. Sed, quamvis multos ornatum verborum quaerere, paucos veritatem scire cognoscamus, nihil de multitudine, sed de paucorum probitate gloriantes, soli veritati insudabimus: maluimus enim promittere nudam veritatem, quam palliatam falsitatem.'
5. 'The society has . . . exacted from its members a close, naked, natural way of speaking; positive expressions; clear senses; a native easiness; bringing all things as near the Mathematical plainness as they can' from Sprat's *History of the Royal Society*, 1667 quoted in Clark's *Seventeenth Century*, p. 336.
6. 'Nos autem dicimus, in omnibus rationem esse quaerendam, si autem alicui deficiat quod divina pagina affirmat, sancto Spiritui et fidei est mandandum . . . quis cum de divinitate aliquid quaerimus, si ad illus comprehendendum non sufficimus, vicinum domui nostrae convocemus, id est manentem in eadem fide catholica inquiramus. Si autem neque, neque ille ad id comprehendendum non sufficimus, tunc igne fidei comburamus. Sed isti vicinos multos habentes domui suae conjunctos, ex superbia nolunt aliquem convocare: maluntque nescire, quam ab alio quaerere.' *Phil.*, I, XXIII.
7. *Phil.*, XLI. 'Quippe cum per cognitionem creaturae ad cognitionem Creatoris perveniamus.'
8. *Eodem*, p. 6. 'Felix, qui potuit rerum cognoscere causas.'
9. Dicis enim ut in domo habitans quilibet, si materiam eius et composionem, quantitatem et qualitatem sive districtionem ignoret, tali hospicio dignus non est ita si qui in aula mundi natus atque educatus est, tam mirande pulchritudinis rationem scire neglegat, post discretionis annos indignus atque si fieri posset exiciendus est. *Astrolabium*, praef. (MS Cambridge, Fitzwilliam Museum, McClean 165, f. 81).

74 The New Conception of Science

10. *Quaes.*, p. 23. 'Non enim intelligis, quia nullum naturale immundum vel indecens est. Quidquid autem contra naturae est, id, licet quantum ad visum picturaliter decoratum sit, in se tamen et immundum et iniquum esse iure dicitur.'

11. '... cum enim universitatis pulchritudinem, caeli terraeque machinam, opus mirabile delectabileque homo inspicit ...' *Liber de stabilitate animae* (PL CCXIII 917).

12. *Glossa* (PL CCXIII 917), p. 104. 'Hac utilitate agi de tali materia tali modo, ut visa potentia divina et sapientia et bonitate in creatione rerum, timeamus tam potentem, veneremur tam sapientiam, diligamus tam benignum.'

13. *Benjamin Major* (PL CXCVI 10, I, 6). '... secundum autem contemplationis genus est quod in imaginatione quidem constitit, secundum rationem tamen formatur atque procedit, quod fit quando ad ea quae in imaginatione versamus ... rationem quaerimus et invenimus, imo inventam et notam inconsiderationem cum admiratione adducimus. In illo atque res ipsas, in isto earum utique rationem, ordinem, dispositionem et uniusque rei causam, modum et utilitatem rimamur, speculamur, miramur.'

14. *Elucid.*, i. 12 (PL CLXXII 1117). 'Omnis atque Dei creatio consideranti magna est delectatio, dum in quibusdam sit decor, ut in floribus; in aliquibus medicina, ut in herbis; inquibusdam pastus, ut in frugibus; in quibusdam significatio, ut in verminibus.'

15. *Quaes.*, p. 10. 'Itaque et ratio procedit et non simul sentimus.'

16. *Quaes.*, pp. 12, 14. 'Stet igitur: inter me et te ratio sola iudex sit ... Quoniam rationabiliter procedis, rationem audi et recipe.'

17. *Quaes.*, p. 6. 'Et quoniam prima quaestio ratione soluta ets, si quid de caeteris ambiguis, propone.'

18. *Quaes.*, p. 25. 'Quoiniam vero de his, quae circa vultum sunt, disserere incepimus, de sensibus ipsis enodandum esse iudico. Nihil enim in corporea hominis compositione meo iudico vel intellectu difficilius vel mutua allocutione inexplicabilius est. Et merito. Dum enim vulgares homines rerum scientias vel falso adscriptione sibi arrogent vel parvipendendas esse iudicent, fit demum, ut in seipsis inveniant quodam, quod disserere nequeant. Unde et Boëthius in Musica de eisdem sensibus ait: "Inter philosophos quidem dubitabile est, vulgus vero dubitatio praeterit." In primis igitur de auditu quid sentias, audiamus.'

19. *Phil.*, XX. 'Hactenus de illis quae sunt, et non videntur nostra disseruit oratio, nunc ad ea quae sunt et videntur, stylus convertatur.'

20. *Dragmaticon*, 28D. Has particulas, quos esse elementa constituis, esse visibiles an invisibiles dicis? Sed si sunt visibiles, non carent divisione; si sunt invisibiles, cum nullo alio sensu percipiantur, quomodo stabit hoc quod dicit Lucretius.

21. *Sermo*, 23 (PL CCV 730A). 'Nam vel *mathematice* speculatur visibiles rerum visibilium causas, vel *physice* invisibiles rerum visibilium causas, vel *symbolice* colligit et coaptat formas visibiles ad invisibilium demonstrationem, vel *theologice* contemplatur invisibiles substantiae et invisibilium substantiarum invisibiles naturas.'

22. See A.C. Crombie, *Grosseteste and Experimental Science* (Oxford, 1953), pp. 22, 23.

23. *Prologus in Eptatheucon*, E. Jeauneau (ed.), in *Medieval Studies*, XVI, no. 4 (1954), pp. 171–5. 'Trivium quadruvio ad generose nationis phylosophorum propaginem quasi maritali federe copulavimus ... Nam, cum sint duo precipua phylosophandi instrumenta, intellectus eiusque interpretatio, intellectum autem quadrivium illuminet, eius vero interpretationem elegantem, rationabilem, ornatam trivium subministret, manifestum est eptatheucon totius phylosophye unicum ac singulare esse instrumentum.'

24. Gundisalvo, *Div. Phil.*, Prol., Baur, (ed.) in *Beiträge Geschichte* etc., Band 4, Heft 2–3 (Munich, 1903) p. 27.

25. 'Empirici vero experienciam solam sectantur; Logici experiencie racionem

adiungunt; Methodici nec elementorum racionem observant, nec tempora nec etates, set solas morborum substancias, et ideo remansit in usu et auctoritate sola racionalis.' Gundisalvo, p. 89.

26. Southern, p. 46.

27. Ibid., p. 81.

28. M. Clagett, Gaines Post and Robert Reynolds (eds), *Twelfth Century Europe and the Foundations of Modern Society* (Madison, 1970), p. 42. Katzenellenbogen writes, '. . . as the second person of the Trinity, the Child enthroned as Godhead incarnate is also Wisdom incarnate . . . The traditional type of *Sedes Sapientiae* (a commonplace topos in the early Middle Ages) gains at Chartres a more specific and profound meaning, because the Wisdom incarnate is related to human wisdom as exemplified by its instruments, that is, the seven Liberal Arts and their representatives, in the archivolts.' Adolf Katzenellenbogen, *The Sculptural Programs of Chartres Cathedral* (New York, 1964), p. 15.

Elsewhere he says, 'The clarity with which actual forms and their arrangement make the idea represented understandable for the intellect . . . show the effect of a great intellectual center . . . The particular protohumanism of the School of Chartres also pervades the iconography . . . The power of reason is strongly and definitely stated in the Liberal Arts but not accorded autonomy. Reason remains dependent and centered on Divine Wisdom . . . The main emphasis is placed on theological truths which are made clear to the mind at the expense of narrative exuberance and emotional intensity.' pp. 47–8.

29. *Eodem*, p. 32. 'Haec enim sua disciplina comprehensam mundi formam, numerum quantitatemque circulorum, distantias orbium, cursus planetarum, situs signorum describit, parallelos colurosque depingit.'

30. *Phil.*, Bk 2. Herman of Carinthia, in his *De essentiis* written in 1143, mingles astronomy with Arabic astrology. On this fuzzy area, see Winthrop Wetherbee, *Platonism and Poetry in the Twelfth Century* (Princeton, 1972).

31. *De operibus sex dierum*, pp. 181, 182.

32. Ibid., p. 180. 'Adsint igitur quatuor genera rationum quae ducunt hominem ad cognitionem creatoris, scilicet arithmeticae probationes et usicae et geometricae et astronomicae, quibus instrumentis in hac theologia breviter utendum set, et ut artificium creatoris in rebus appareat et quod proposuimus rationabiliter ostendatur.'

33. A.C. Crombie, *Grosseteste*, pp. 23–4. 'According to Aristotle, scientific investigation and explanation was a two-fold process, the first inductive, the second deductive. Beginning with facts observed through the senses, [one] must ascend by induction to generalisations or universal forms or causes which were most remote from sensory experience . . . The second process in science was to descend again by deduction from these universal forms to the observed facts which were thus explained by being demonstrated from prior and more general principles which were their cause.'

34. For a thorough account of the history of these development, see A.C. Crombie, *Augustine to Galileo: Science in the Middle Ages* (London, 1970).

35. *Phil.*, Lib. 2, III, 58. 'Ut autem verbis rustici utar, potest Deus facere de trunco vitulum: fecitne unquam? Vel igitur ostendant rationem, vel utilitatem ad quam hoc sit, vel sic esse indicare desinant.'

In the *Dragmaticon*, William writes: 'Quid est stultius quam affirmare aliquid, quia creator potest illud facere? Facitne quicquid potest? Qui igitur Deum aliquid contra naturam facere dicit, vel sic esse oculis videtur, vel rationem quare hoc sit ostendat, vel utilitatem ad quam hoc sit praetendat.' VI.

36. *Quaes.*, p. 57. 'Omnium quidem habitudo sensuum, (ut Boëthius in Musica testatur) omnibus animalibus praesto est. Sed quae eorundem sit vis quisve modus, nonnisi intellectui philosophantis perspicuum est praeclare. Nam et rerum effectus nexu subtilissimo a causi praecedentibus procedunt et ipsae inter se causae cum suit

effectibus subtilissimis quibusdam interstitiis differunt, unde et ipsis philosophis rerum natura saepe se subtrahit.'

37.   Clagett, 'Aspects of Physics', p. 34.

38.   Hugh of St Victor, *Erud. Didasc.*, ii, 17 (Taylor trans.) 'What is essential to mathematics is that, given a set of premises, the conclusion will follow it in all cases. For pedagogic or administrative purposes it may still be necessary to refrain from identifying mathematics with the whole region of necessary inferences in which all exact science is located, but in point of fact, there is no strictly logical difference between pure mathematics and deductive reasoning.' *A Preface to Logic*, Morris R. Cohen (London, 1946), p. 10.

39.   *Glossulae super Porphyrium*, quoted in A.C. Crombie, *Grosseteste* (Oxford, 1953), p. 30.

Peter Abelard helped to direct the rationalist movement towards the investigation of nature, and his contribution towards a scientific method may be summarised as follows: (1) the notion of a scientific scepticism; (2) learn to discriminate between scientific statements that provide rational proof from those that are merely persuasive; (3) cultivate precision in terminology, whether in reading others' statements or formulating your own; (4) keep a sharp eye out for errors in traditional writings, even in the Bible or Church Fathers (see especially his Introduction to *Sic et Non*).

Abelard's epitaph is attributed to Peter the Venerable, Abbot of Cluny: 'Omnia vi superans rationis et art loquendi/Abaelardus erat . . .' Abelard, *Opera*, Victor Cousin (ed.), Vol. I (Paris, 1849), p. 717.

40.   Crombie, *Grosseteste*, p. 30.

41.   *Eodem*, p. 28. '. . . Graeci geometriam a terrae comprehendit? . . . Quis item atomi parvitatem oculo distinxit?'

42.   Et meo certe iudicio in hoc sensibili mundo nihil omnino moritur, nec minor est hodie quam cum creatus est. Si quam enim pars ab una coniunctione solvitur, non perit, sed ad aliam societatem transit.' *Quaestiones*, 4, 20.

43.   Crombie, *Grosseteste*, p. 13.

44.   *Eodem*, p. 13. 'Quis enim unquam caeli spatium visu comprehendit? . . . Quis item atomi parvitatem oculo distinxit?'

45.   Ibid., p. 13. 'Unde nec ex sensibus scientia, sed opinio oriri valet. Hinc est, quod familiaris meus Plato sensus irrationabiles vocat.'

46.   Ibid., p. 13. 'O perverso rerum conversio, cum nihil ratione certius, nihil sensibus fallacius!'

Dyksterhuis quotes Mach: '*die Sinne lügen nicht sie sagen nur nicht die Wahrheit*', *The Mechanization of the World Picture*, p. 133.

47.   'Est enim natura caloris aquam in minutissimas guttas dividere et eas minutas virtute sui motus super aera elevare sicut in fumo caldarii apparet: sicut etiam in nubibus celi manifestum est.' Ibid., 7.

48.   Ibid., p. 174.

49.   The cosmologists were well aware of the principle: *nihil est in intellectu quod non prius fuerit in sensu*. See Crombie, 'The significance of Medieval Discussions of scientific method for the scientific Revolution', in Clagett, *Critical Problems* (Madison, 1959), pp. 79–101.

50.   Crombie, *Grosseteste*, p. 11.

51.   Ibid.

52.   See P. Wiener and A. Noland (eds), *Roots of Scientific Thought* (New York, 1960), pp. 125–38.

53.   Galen's work, *Metalegni (Therapeutica)*, iii, f. 190 became available in the West in the late eleventh century through translations by Constantinus Africanus. On the study of disease he says: '. . . eam cum experimento invenire investigamus . . . Sicut enim experimentum sine ratione est debile, sic et ratio noniuncta experimento fallax est . . . Experimento autem necessarium est longum tempus cum tentatione rei.'

54. *Glossa in Timaeum*, p. 104. 'Ostenso quod nichil est sine causa, sub iungit quid contrahat effectus ex efficiente. Et sciendum quod omne opus vel est opus Creatoris, vel opus natura, vel artificis imitantis naturam. Et est opus natura, vel artificis imitantis naturam. Et est opus Creatoris prima creatio sine preiacente materia . . . Opus nature est quod similia nascuntur ex similibus, ex semine vel ex germine. Et est natura vis rebus insit similia de similibus operans. Opus artificis est opus hominis quod propter indigentiam operatur ut vestimenta contra frigus, domum contra aeris.'

55. Ibid.

56. John James, *The Contractors of Chartres* (Wyong, 1981), I, p. 235. Elsewhere James says, 'Geometry pervades the entire building, from the largest element to the smallest.' II, p. 552.

57. See *Meta.*, II, 11, 42B and II, 13, 870D.

58. *Quaes.*, p. 57. 'Immo, quod minime putas, in hoc maxime rerum ordinem naturaeque rationem servat.'

59. The idea originated in Plato. (See Pierre Duhem, *To Save the Phenomena, an Essay on the Idea of Physical Theory from Plato to Galileo* trans. E. Dolard and C. Maschler (University of Chicago, 1969).)

60. *Eodem*, pp. 5, 6. 'Alius enim a sensibilibus investigandas esse censuit, alter ab insensibilibus incepit; alius eas etiam esse divinavit . . . Aiunt enim nullam esse certificationem sensuum, nec oculis nec auribus ceterisque credendum esse . . . Utinamque omnes caeci surdique efficiantur!'

61. This problem, although commented upon by Haskins, Thorndike and Crombie has not been adequately explored; it is customary to credit Grosseteste and Bacon with initiating the formulation of scientific attitudes and methodology. Crombie credits the Oxford group, beginning with Grosseteste with being first to present a coherent methodology, 'in particular the study of the relation between theory and experience, of the use of induction and experiment in scientific investigation, of the relation of mathematical to "physical" and metaphysical explanations, and of the problem of certainty in the study of the world known through the senses . . . With Grosseteste, Oxford became the first center of the methodological revolution with which modern science began.' Crombie, *Grosseteste*, p. 14.

62. *Entheticus* (PL 199, 1978).
Causarum series natura vocatur, ab illa
Sensilis hic mundus contrahit esse suum.
Et si vicinis concordant plasmata causis,
Tunc natura parens omne figurat opus.
Si sit ab eventu vicino dissona causa,
Contra naturam turba quid esse putat
Et quia causa latet, dicit naturam carere:
Sed plane nihil est quod ratione caret.

63. 'qui causas occultas rerum comprehendere ac deliberare valet'. *Philosophische Schriften*, Geyer (ed.), *Beiträge*, etc. XXI (Münster, 1933), pp. 1–4.

64. 'Dubitando enim ad inquisitionem venimus, inquirendo veritatem percipimus.' Ibid., p. 202.

65. *Quaes.*, pp. 58–9. 'Quid est, quod ipsum totum usque adeo admireris? Quid stupes, quid dubites? Quid nunc hac, nunc illac nutans, inconstantiae vultum praestas? Atqui scio, qua tenebra teneris, quae universos, qui de rerum ordine dubitant, involvit et in errorum inducit. Admiratione enim insolentiaque indutus animus, dum rerum effectus sine causis abhorrens a longe aspicit, nunquam se dubitatione exuit. Propius intuere, circumstantias adde, causas propone, et effectum non mirabere. Ne sis ille, qui mavult nescire, quam accedere! Tales nempe in hac sententia fere omnes repperi. Unde, sum eis aliquid tale promitto, nec promittentem recipiunt, nec explicantem audiunt, meque digito ostendunt et insaniam mihi imponunt.'

4 The Critical Examination of Tradition

If it was difficult for twelfth-century Europeans to accustom themselves to looking critically at experience, it was perhaps, even harder to accept the cosmologists' attack on tradition. What was attacked was not the body of tradition but the unquestioned acceptance of it typical of the day. In a culture remarkable for its cohesiveness, the solidity of its intellectual foundations was equally remarkable, so that an attack on the *auctores* — those whose writings comprised the body of tradition — was indeed an audacious act.

Adelard of Bath is ironic about his era's supine dependence upon tradition.

> This generation has an innate voice, namely, that it can accept nothing which has been discovered by contemporaries; as a consequence, when I wish to publish something I myself have discovered, I ascribe it to someone else, saying 'a certain man (not I) has said' . . .[2]

Peter Abelard thought that 'Authority is inferior to reason because it deals with opinions about the truth rather than with truth itself, while reason concerns the thing itself and can settle the question.'[2] Abelard does not want to take his knowledge secondhand if it can be avoided; he does not discount authority, but only its uncritical acceptance. Adelard of Bath is less temperate in his view of the danger of depending on authority.

> For authority alone cannot create belief in the thought of a philosopher nor even lead one towards such belief, and this is why logicians agree that citing authority does not even necessarily add probability to a given argument. So if you wish to hear more from me, give and take reason. For I am not a man who can satisfy his hunger from a picture of a steak! Indeed, all letters is a whore, influenced by and displaying the same emotion now towards this one, now towards another![3]

He is shrewd enough to see that citing an authority, however great, cannot add a jot to the likeliness or plausibility of a theory, unless it is logically valid in itself.

William of Conches expresses exactly the same idea:

> It is not lawful to speak against any matter concerning either the Catholic faith or Church regulations, nor be aroused in opposition to men [such as] the Venerable Bede or other holy Fathers; however, in those matters concerning philosophy, if they err in any respect, it is permissible to differ from them. For even though they were greater men than we are, yet they were men.[4]

This critical stance was a prerequisite for the fledgling scientist of the twelfth century, for there were serious problems standing in the way of sustained progress: the relatively low standard of many kinds of technical skill and of precise knowledge (e.g. mathematics); the difficulty of perceiving the peculiar and distinctive character of natural science; and the general attitude of students of science towards seeking scientific truth. Dyksterhuis says:

> ... we have to appreciate the awe for the authority of tradition in which the medieval thinkers had been brought up, and to realise that this dominated the sphere of natural knowledge just as strongly as that of religion ... Natural science was not viewed as something which constantly has to be acquired anew, which incessantly has to be elaborated further; men were convinced that it already existed [like the medieval view of law as found not made], or at any rate had once existed, and that the problem was to recover it.[5]

This awe of the authority of tradition included a very natural respect for the august *auctores* — the Church Fathers and the ancients, whose judgments on all subjects, religious or other, were held in the highest regard. Quoting the *auctores* in support of an opinion on any matter was so much the approved procedure among scholars in the middle ages that doing so came to constitute the usual means of proving the truth of a statement. The rationalist attitude of the period made for controversy between autonomous reason and authority, and this controversy entered a new phase when an interest in a physical explanation for the universe (*secundum physicam*) intensified. 'Without being directed against religious faith, "scientific" reasoning inevitably extended its scope and aspired to ever greater autonomy.'[6]

In the twelfth century then, it came to be felt that a vigorous campaign must be fought against a blind reliance on authority as a preliminary step towards encouraging scientific study. Alan of Lille understood this need: 'But since an authority has a nose made of wax, it is possible to twist it in any direction, so that one must rely on strengthening the rational faculty.'[7] This argument was put to good use by the cosmologists and is heard often in various forms during the century.

Adelard well knows his period's propensity to abdicate one's own critical faculty in favour of trusting implicitly the judgment of an ancient authority:

> For I was taught by my Arab masters to be led only by reason, whereas you were taught to follow the halter of the captured image of authority. For what else can such authority be but a halter? Indeed, as brute animals are led in their halters and can perceive neither the direction nor the purpose of their journey, they can only follow the rope by which they are led — nor can they see who is pulling them. In like manner, your students have been captured and enchained in a similar bestial credulity, and led into dangerous paths by these written authorities. An example of this danger is when men usurp the name of an authority to write with expressive freedom themselves, and do this to such a point that they do not hesitate to put falsehood before truth ... There are so many students who do not question the reason behind the judgment they are accepting, but prefer to trust in an ancient name. For they do not perceive that for true judgment, reason is given to everyone so that each might distinguish between the false and the true. And unless reason is adopted as the universal mode of judging problems concerning nature, in vain will you try to impart knowledge to your students. For if you teach the authorities' writing either to one alone or to many, most of your students, I believe, will be merely content to accept the established and traditional views. Moreover, of these figures whom we accept as authorities, none of them ought to be believed by students except to the extent that they are clearly following reason — to the degree that they fail to do this, either through ignorance or negligence, these authorities deserve to be regarded as obscure, unclear! However, I don't mean to belabour the point — that all authority is to be subject to the reader's own best judgment. But I believe that reason should be sought first of all, and authority — if added at all — should be subordinate to it.[8]

What science there was before the mid-eleventh century could develop independently of the body of Christian doctrine, because it did not concern itself with questions that impinged upon this doctrine. However, by the time the cosmologists were writing, the entire structure of the natural world had begun to come under the scrutiny of scientists, and the boundaries of science and theology became less distinct. Guy Beaujouan warns us not to overemphasise the rationalist impulse of the twelfth century. He mentions that Thierry's biblical commentary does not claim to be compelling as proofs but rather were, as he says 'intellectual steps toward consolidating the Faith'. I cannot agree, however, that the impulse to set forth *probationes* expressed by Anselm, Thierry of Chartres and the other cosmologists was a response to any perceptible weakening of the Christian faith in this period. I see it purely as a powerful need to harness the intellect in the service of all experience, including religion. It is a curious fact that for a brief moment, in this period, science and religion showed unmistakable signs of approaching an accommodation that might eventually have proved stable and dependable.

In the first place, from the time of Berengar, the possible application of the art of dialectic to the study of theology was considered. After Anselm, the movement to rationalise theology gained momentum, and as it became common for men to attempt to order every kind of knowledge as a system of deductions like mathematics, starting from undemonstrable first principles and proceeding to the proposition to be demonstrated, some began to apply this method to theology. A concomitant of the increased interest in a rational theology was a need to come to terms with the question of the relation between the study of natural science and the study of theology. One way to reconcile them was to regard reason as a valuable aid in tracing the craftsmanship of the Creator and to see its highest function as seeking knowledge of the causes of things in the service of God.[9]

The scientists of the early twelfth century offered tentative suggestions regarding the occurrence of miracles in a universe tightly governed by rational laws. William of Conches sees that 'the world is an ordered aggregation of creatures'.[10] He tries to clarify the rational principles underlying nature and at the same time account for the possibility of God's acting outside it. In his commentary on Plato's *Timaeus* he writes:

Having shown that nothing exists without a cause, Plato now narrows the discussion to the distinguishing of effect from efficient cause. It must be recognised that every work is the work of the *Creator*, or of *Nature*, or the work of a human artisan imitating nature. The work of the Creator is the first creation without pre-existing material, for example the creation of the elements or spirits, or it is the things we see happen contrary to the accustomed course of nature, as the virgin birth and the like.[11]

This statement about God's power to contravene nature's causal principles occurs, significantly, in a late work which was probably written long after the *De philosophia mundi* — a work censured by the Church for its daring unorthodoxy on the subject of miracles and other matters. (See Chapter 2.) Peter Abelard also tried to deal with the point at which nature's powers and God's diverge:

Perhaps someone will ask too, by what power of nature this came to be. First, I will reply that when we require to assign the power of nature or natural causes to certain effects of things, we by no means do so in a manner resembling God's first operation in constituting the world, when only the will of God had the force of nature in creating things . . . We go on to examine the power of nature . . . so that the constitution or development of everything that originates without miracles can be adequately accounted for.[12]

William of Conches was at some pains to reserve for God all due praise for the creation of man while giving to nature the credit for effecting the generation of men.

Someone will allege that this [the idea of nature's being responsible for the generation of men] is to derogate from the divine power. To such we shall reply that, on the contrary, it adds to the divine power because to that power we attribute not only the giving of a productive nature of things but the creation of the human body through the operation of such nature.[13]

Although the critical attitude towards authorities cultivated by the cosmologists did not extend to Scripture, it was inevitable that these men would find themselves extending their new mental habit of critical analysis to those portions of Genesis which offered an account of the creation of the world. Thierry of Chartres introduced his commentary on the first chapter of this book: 'This is an exegetical study of the first portion of Genesis from the point of view of an investigator of natural processes [*secundum physicam*] and of the literal meaning of the text.'[14] This simple statement of intention was of historic importance, for it was the first conscious and deliberate attempt to analyse a part of the Bible as a scientist, a man in search of rational explanations, for the only account of the origins of the universe known to the twelfth century except for the account given in the *Timaeus*.

Resolutely, Thierry commences his study, 'In the beginning God created the heaven and the earth', and then proceeds in the way he has set himself to go:

> ... as if he might say: he first created heaven and earth. For he wanted another to understand through this statement, that when he said 'In the beginning he created', it is to be understood that he created nothing prior to these and that this act was the creation of these two entities simultaneously. But I will attempt to demonstrate both what is meant by 'heaven' and 'earth', and also show the manner of this coming into being of these natural phenomena in accordance with reason.[15]

Thierry goes on to explain that Moses' purpose in writing this book was to show how God alone accomplished his great task and so carried it out as to illustrate perfectly his own wisdom. This universe then, is necessarily so constructed as to exhibit in the highest degree a rational and beautiful order. This beauty and this logic (*rationalabiliter*) exist in consequence of God's paramount wisdom. When Moses, for example, says 'In the beginning ...' what he literally means is that the first thing that God created was actually matter — the basic substratum of things, that include four elements: fire, air, earth and water. Afterwards, by a natural process, matter took on distinguishable forms and in these forms the four elements were put in motion.[16]

From this account of a portion of Thierry's work, it is possible to discern his mode of operation. Bit by bit he works his way through the sacred text, explicating each statement *secundum physicam rationes* with highly original and ingenious interpretations which confidently offer a logical explanation of each point. Thierry presents the concept of a chain of causality in the entire process of creation from primordial matter to its most complex form, man; his purpose is to bring out the logical and, so to speak, automatic nature of the creation of the world. There is something resembling the notion of a chain reaction which got under way after God performed the initial act of creating the primal matter. 'Reason' continues to produce in nature the whole, complex cosmos that God envisioned before He acted. In the combining and mutual reacting of the elements of basic matter, Thierry sees the mechanism of a continual creation (or development) occurring in time — a theory similar to current theories on the chemical beginnings of life. He postulates transformations of matter in the direction of increasing differentiation from a thoroughly mixed state to clearly discrete entities.

Thierry of Chartres, according to Nicolas Häring, was a powerful and independent thinker. Häring says, 'A close study of Thierry's sources generally confirms the impression that he was indeed a keen thinker [and] an original writer.'[17] Häring believes the commentary to be unequalled in the history of exegesis. Pierre Duhem speaks of Thierry's *audace rationaliste*'.[18] Dyksterhuis says of Thierry, '. . . he wants to give a physical explanation of the way in which everything originated, and to this end he follows the guidance of the *Timaeus . . .* This physical theory of creation is based on the action of intrinsic forces of nature . . .'[19]

William of Conches also took on portions of the Bible for scrutinising in a scientific manner. His comments are as cogent as Thierry's, but his manner is less organised; he has no wish to cover everything on nature systematically. When he is unable to make the biblical statement yield a reasonable explanation he says so:

> . . . and the divine pages say, 'He divided the waters which were under the firmament from the waters which were above the firmament.' But since this is against reason [*contra rationem*] its cause cannot be shown by us, nor can we explain just how that statement is to be understood.[20]

Elsewhere he writes, '. . . the divine scriptures tell us that God created man from the dirt of the earth; but this must not be believed — that the mind which is quasi-divine, light and elegant was made from dirt.'[21] And again:

> . . . the divine pages say that woman was made from the side of Adam. This too, is not to be believed literally [*ad litteram*], nor does it tally with the account of the first man. It might be said by some that if that statement is meant literally, why were many men and women not created by that method, and why can't they be still? We would say that God is capable — has the power through the

operation of his divine will — to effect such a deed. However, we maintain that divine power always operates through nature; so that while we admit the fact of God's will operating, we say that whatever can be described as a function of nature, such functioning is necessarily by virtue of a preliminary (or preceding) operation of the divine will. Others might object that such a view is in effect a limiting of God's power — to say that the generation of man is in accordance with natural functioning. To this objection we reply — on the contrary, we are thereby actually adding to the scope of God's will: first in attributing to him the giving of great capacities to nature in general, and second, for the unique skill of nature in the creation of the human body. But if we explain how something that the Bible tells us happened, did happen — how are we going against the divine scripture? . . . But since those same persons who argue against our view are themselves totally ignorant of the forces of nature [*vires naturae*], they consider, as the result of their ignorance, that all their colleagues are equally lacking in knowledge. They have consequently, no desire to inquire anything at all of them. But they behave, rather, as our rustics (peasants) do — they simply believe, and they do not bother to seek the natural reason thus fulfilling the prophet (Isaiah: XXIV) 'And the people were themselves priests' . . . These people really prefer not to know rather than ask of another [who is willing to search for natural causes]. Therefore they are quick to shout 'heretics' of those inquirers, having more faith in their preconceptions than in their ability to think independently.[22]

The view of William of Conches that the creation of Eve was effected through the action of natural forces on matter, similar (but not identical) to that of which Adam was composed opened the scientist to the charge of naturalism, the theory that nature works independently of God. William avoided the charge by saying that nature's capacity to function was a divine gift. He thought that one ought not to invoke God's omnipotence in giving scientific explanations. Dyksterhuis sees William's view of the working relationship between God and nature as far more rational and direct than the later Averroist theory and the 'corrected' form of it worked out in the next century. Had William's contemporaries accepted it, it is reasonable to suppose that a far wider interest in science would have been the result.[23]

Medieval men inherited from Augustine a Christian tradition

which encouraged a consideration of the nature of things, and consequently Western Christendom was predisposed to value the natural world as sacramental and symbolic of Christian truths. By the twelfth century, however, some men had begun to realise that the study of natural causes had a legitimate interest of its own quite apart from this world's emblematic function. Before William of Conches, Adelard of Bath was aware that the scientific approach must differ from the theological, that natural philosophy must invent a different set of concepts to express an important distinction of thought.

William of Conches is eager to defend his literal examination of statements in Genesis and devises an argument which advances a distinction between God's power to create, or do anything He wills, and the extent of natural forces (*vires naturae*). 'But someone will say, "Isn't it the Creator's work that man is born from man?" To which I reply, "I do not mean to detract from God's powers."'[24] To draw a line between the two kinds and degrees of power is not easy, and many failed to comprehend it; William loses patience with those men and hotly chastises them for ignorance and arrogance. Neither William nor Thierry is able to convince their critics, and the meagre evidence we have suggests that the critics gain the upper hand and eventually bring them to their knees. Meanwhile, William writes derisively of the enemies of the new science.

> But when modern priests hear this, they ridicule it immediately because they do not find it in the Bible. They don't realise that the authors of truth are silent on matters of natural philosophy, not because these matters are against the faith, but because they have little to do with the strengthening of such faith, which is what those authors are concerned with. But modern priests do not want us to inquire into anything that isn't in the Scriptures, only to believe simply, like peasants.[25]

Elsewhere William says that it is not the purpose of the Bible to teach us about nature but of philosophy. Again, he asks: 'How are we contrary to the divine Scriptures if, concerning that which it states to have been done, we explain the manner in which it was done?'[26] Peter Abelard comments, 'Whatever they do not understand they call foolishness; whatever they cannot grasp they judge to be insanity.'[27] Peter Abelard himself demurs at using reason as a warrant for belief in Christian doctrine: '. . . [reason] is not something which gives an intellectual justification of faith which we have on other grounds.'[28]

But elsewhere Abelard supports William of Conches in his argument concerning science as adding to, rather than subtracting from, divine power.

The problem of establishing a division between divine power and nature's forces was peculiarly relevant to medieval concerns because it involved the validating of the occurrence of miracles. We saw how the twelfth-century scientists at times clearly delimited the study of nature from the larger and more central subject, theology. The earliest of the cosmologists, Adelard of Bath, felt sufficient confidence in nature's basic rationality to say:

Wherefore, [since a wise God is unwilling to abolish the orderly workings of nature] it is not even possible for such a change of position [relating to the idea that nature is not ordered], and among philosophers it is agreed that any upsetting of this spirit of order is least likely to occur.[29]

An occasional indignant diatribe against the new science can still be found to give us an idea of what the cosmologists were up against. 'Let no one impiously think, as certain impious men have, that things contrary to nature — that is, contrary to the accustomed course of nature — cannot occur,' writes an anonymous monk.[30] Absolom of St Victor roundly condemned this prying into the 'composition of the globe, the nature of the elements, the location of the stars, the nature of animals, the violence of the wind, the life-processes of plants and of roots.'[31] The metaphysician William of St Thierry was outspoken in his total rejection of and deep hostility towards the work of the men promoting the new science.

As to the creation of woman from the rib of Adam, [William of Conches] holds the authority of the sacred history in contempt . . .; by interpreting that history from the point of view of physical science, he arrogantly prefers the ideas he invents to the truth the history contains, and in so doing he makes light of a great mystery.[32]

Another time he writes:

Moreover, after the theology of Peter Abelard, William of Conches produced a new philosophy, confirming and strengthening whatever the former had said; and with greater impudence adding to it much of his own which Abelard had not said, his [William's] worthless innovations.[33]

Some degree of persecution was experienced by Thierry of Chartres as well as by William of Conches and Peter Abelard; long after Thierry had been forced out of his teaching position, he wrote bitterly, 'Ecce Theodoricus Brito — homo barbaricae nationis, verbi insulus, corpore ac mente incompositus, mendacem de se te vocat . . .'[34]

Huizinga has commented that 'The life of the schools in the twelfth century was one of competition and heated controversies, one of envy and slander, contumely and libel;'[35] and from the words of Thierry of Chartres and William of Conches, this was especially true of men who tried to teach the new science. We know from John of Salisbury's account of William's teaching career that it was increasingly hard going:

> . . . but afterwards [following a long teaching career] when opinion did prejudice to truth, and men chose rather to seem than to be philosophers, and professors of arts undertook to instill the whole of philosophy into their auditors more quickly then — in three or even two years — they were overcome by the onset of the unskilled crowd and retired.[36]

Thierry of Chartres suffered much from hostile students and envious colleagues; here he gives vent to his resentment:

> As Petronius says, we masters shall be left alone in the schools unless we flatter the multitude and trap them into listening. But I do not accept this state of affairs . . . I have so limited my class that I exclude the common herd [*vulgus profanum*] and the hodge-podge audience of a school.[37]

We know from a Latin lyric of the day that Thierry was feared for his 'sharp tongue that cut like a sword'.[38] We sense his despair when he writes, 'Fame . . . accuses Thierry everywhere, calls him ignominious names . . . a necromancer and a heretic.'[39]

William of Conches writes thoughtfully of his teaching problems; we see that he has analysed the situation with care and much seriousness:

> He who teaches ought to be a certain kind of man, one whose

teaching is motivated neither by the desire for praise nor the hope of temporal payments, but solely by the love of wisdom. For if he declines in his own praise, he will never wish to bring his pupil up to his own degree of perfection in knowledge. Consequently, he will teach less than he knows so as to prevent his pupil becoming equal or superior to him. On the other hand, if he is led by the hope of temporal remuneration — provided that he can extort money — he will not take pains with his work because his mind will be taken up with getting money. And more often he will please by teaching nonsense or trifles, than by teaching what is of use. But the right kind of teacher approaches his work through the love of knowledge. He does not attempt to subvert his subject-matter through his own hostility towards the one who produced the material, nor does he attempt to force his teaching on his students. He never flees from true knowledge, never fails to support his many fellow teachers but rather will be zealous and watchful in the preparation and presentation of his own work and also towards the work of others.[40]

We have here, by inference, an accurate picture of master, student and colleagues involved in the process of education in the cathedral schools in mid-century — a picture that must have been particularly descriptive of classes where science was taught.

William of Conches was deeply convinced of the value of his profession, and in the following exerpt we see that then — as now — most young men did not agree.

The ideal student is one who does not disturb the class, is not arrogant and does not pretend to a degree of intelligence beyond his real capacity. Such a student will value his master as he does his own father — or even more than his father. For though we will accept as much dignity as is due the father, in fact we ought to receive more than that: though one accepts ignorance from one's father, one receives wisdom from one's teacher and wisdom is more valuable and worthy of respect. Therefore one ought to esteem good masters more highly than parents.[41]

This passage has an undertone of resentment, expressed ironically, and we wonder whether his readers were shocked by it. The following portion reveals the extent of William's frustration and anger at the sorry state of things in his classroom:

Now are the words of the Bible fulfilled: 'For the time will come when they will not endure sound doctrine; but after their own lusts shall they heap to themselves teaching having itching ears' (II Tim. IV, 3). For in the above chapters [in his scientific treatise] which descends from considering the origins of the universe down to that concerning the earth, there is nothing to satisfy the itching ears; but there is much to profit the serious student — consequently the mind of the stupid student will not be suited. Therefore, what freedom of study can be expected of the rest of the students? In a situation where teachers are busy flattering their students and all rules of orderly speaking and remaining silent are without force? Many students take in the expression, voice and look of the flattering teacher, and although some might follow a teacher of severe mien, such a teacher will be shunned by the many fickle students as mad, and he will be called cruel and inhuman . . .'[41]

William is especially enraged by those colleagues who, for the sake of a cheap popularity with their students, will forsake the standards they presumably once had, to truckle to the ignorant.

The careers of some of the cosmologists ended in discouragement, but the attitudes and approaches towards the investigation of nature remained more or less in the air in the following period. To these lovers of science must surely be given much credit for the development of the intellectual movement historians have called humanism: the respect for nature as something worth understanding and appreciating, and the concomitant recognition of the inherent worth and nobility of natural man, an integral part of the created world. Southern speaks of this

. . . strong sense of the dignity of human nature . . . [asserting] not only that man is the noblest of God's creatures, but also that his nobility continues even in his fallen state, that it is capable of development in this world, that the instruments exist by which it can be developed, and that it should be the chief aim of human endeavour to perfect these instruments.[43]

Hence, implicit in the twelfth-century view of nature is the belief in the ability of the human mind to move towards a fuller use of the reasoning faculty, towards a future of increasing knowledge of man, his world and his God. Such a belief, expressed by the cosmologists in many ways, both implicitly and explicitly — such a trust in the progress in knowledge, basic to sustained scientific enterprise — is summed up in the apophthegm of Bernard of Chartres. (See Chapter V, p. 96.) A firm belief in progress almost always accompanies advancement in science. After 1250, when Western Europe had assimilated Aristotelian and Arabic science, Southern says '. . . the main ideas of the earlier masters — the dignity of man, the intelligibility of the universe, the nobility of nature — not only remained intact, but were fundamental concepts in the intellectual structures of the thirteenth century.'[44] Thomas Aquinas, for example, refers often to the value of natural rights and the worth of the faculty of reason.

Although in the century and a half that followed the death of the cosmologists there was a pronounced change towards a more unified and systematic treatment of knowledge — expressed, for example in the many *summae*, the basic role of the rational faculty in man's life remained prominent. In the greatest literary masterpiece of the middle ages, Dante's *Commedia*, this point is everywhere apparent. In his analysis of the work, Bernard Stambler says:

> That the actions chosen by Dante for depiction in the *Commedia* equal all possible actions depends not so much on the commonality or universality of medieval experience as it does on the medieval idea of the world as rational, an idea worked out by Dante to its farthest reaches as the basis for his poem: whatever is has meaning — *post hoc* is always in the deepest sense, and rightly understood, *propter hoc*.[45]

Notes

1. *Quaes.*, *Prolog.*, p. 1. 'Habet enim haec generatio ingenitum vitium, ut nihil, quod a modernis reperiatur, putet esse recipiendum. Unde fit, ut si quando inventum proprium publicare voluerim, personae id, alienae imponens inquam: "Quidam dixit, non ego."'

2. 'Dialogus inter Christianum, Judaeum et Philosophum', as quoted by A. Victor Murray, *Abelard and St. Bernard: A Study in Twelfth-Century 'Modernism'* (New York, 1967), p. 155.

3. *Quaes.*, p. 12. 'Amplius, ipsi, qui auctores vocantur, non aliunde primam fidem apud minores adepti sunt, nisi quia rationem secuti sunt, quam quicunque nesciunt vel negligunt, merito caeci habendi sunt. Neque tamen id ad vivum reseco, ut auctoritas me iudice spernenda sit. Id autem assero, quod prius ratio inquirenda sit, ea inventa auctoritas, si adiacet, demum subdenda . . . Quare si quid amplius a me audire desideras, rationem refer et recipe. Non enim ego ille sum, quem pellis pictura pascere possit. Omnis quippe littera meretrix est, nunc ad hoc ad illos affectus exposita.'

4. *Dragmaticon*, 65, 66. 'In eis quae ad fidem catholicam vel ad morum

institutionem pertinent, non est fas Bedae vel acui alii sanctorum patrum (citra Scripturae Sacrae autoritatem) contradicere: in eis tamen quae ad philosophiam pertinent, si in aliquo errant, licet diversum adfirmare. Etsi enim maiores nobis, homines tamen fuere.'

5.   Dyksterhuis, *The Mechanization of the World Picture*, pp. 116, 117.

6.   M. Clagett, G. Post and R. Reynolds, *Twelfth Century Europe*, p. 12.

7.   'Sed quia auctoritas cereum habet nasum, i.e., in diversum potest flecti sensum, rationibus roborandum est.' *Contra Haereticos*, I, 30.

8.   *Quaes.*, pp. 11–12. 'Ego enim aliud a magistris Arabicis ratione duce didici, tu vero aliud auctoritatis pictura captus capistrum sequeris. Quid enim aliud auctoritas dicenda est quam capistrum? Ut bruta quippe animalia capistro quolibet ducuntur, nec quo aut quare ducantur, discernunt restemque, quo tenetur, solum sepuuntur, sic non paucos vestrum bestiali credulitate captos ligatosque auctoritas scriptorum in periculum ducit. Unde et quidam nomen sibi auctoritas usurpantes nimia scribendi licentia usi sunt, adeo ut pro veris falsa bestialibus viris insinuare non dubitaverunt. Cur enim chartas non impleas, cur et a tergo non scribas, cum tales fere huis temporis auditores habeas, qui nullam iudicii rationem exigant tituli tantum nomine vetusti confidant . . . Amplius, ipsi, qui auctores vocantur, non aliunde primam fidem apud minores adepti sunt, nisi quia rationem secuti sunt, quam quicunque nesciunt vel negligunt, merito caeci habendi sunt. Neque tamen id ad vivum reseco, ut auctoritas me iudice spernenda sit. Id autem assero, quod prius ratio inquirenda sit, ea inventa auctoritas, si adiacet, demum subdenda.'

9.   William of Conches took pains to consider human knowledge, e.g. science, in relation to Divine Wisdom: '"Sapientia huius mundi, stultitia est apud Deum" (I Cor. 1, 20): non quia Deus sapientiam huius mundi reputet, sed quia ad comparationem Dei sapientiae, stultitia est: nec inde ideo sequitur quod sit stultitia.' *Phil.* XIX.

10.   *Glossa in Timaeum*, p. 125. '. . . et est mundus ordinata collectio creaturorum'.

11.   Ibid., see Chapter 3, ns 55 and 56.

12.   'Forte et hoc aliquis requirit . . . qua vi naturae id factum sit. Ad quod primium respondeo nullatenus nos modo, cum in aliquibus rerum effectis vim naturae vel causas naturalis requirimus vel assignamus, id nos facere secundum illam priorem Dei operationem in constitutione mundi ubi sola Dei voluntas naturae efficaciam habuit in illis tunc creandis . . . Deinceps vim naturae pensare solemus . . . ut ad quaelibet sine miraculis facienda illa eorum constitutio vel praeparatio sufficeret.' Peter Abelard, *Expos. in Hexaemeron* 'De secunda die' (PL CLXXVIII 746).

13.   *Phil.*, Lib. 1, XXIII. In his *Glossa in Timaeum*, William has this to say: 'Sed dicit aliquis eadem natione plures homines adhuc cotidie posse creari. Nos dicimus verum esse si divina esset voluntas quia, ut aliquid sit natura operante, necesse est divinam voluntatem precedere. Iterum dicet hoc esse divine potentie derogare sic hominem esse ei conferre quia ei attribuimus et talem rebus naturam dedisse et per naturam operantem corpus humanum creasse.' p. 122. (See fn. 23.)

14.   *De operibus*, p. 172. 'De septem diebus et sex operum distinctionibus primam Geneseos partem secundum physicam et ad litteram ego expositurus, in primus de intentione auctoris et de libri utilitate pauca praemittam, postea vero ad sensum litterae historialem exponendum veniam, ut allegoricam et moralem lectionem, quas sancti expositores aperte exsecuti sunt, ex toto praetermittam.'

15.   Ibid., pp. 172, 177. 'Causas ex quibus habeat mundus existere et temporum ordinem in quibus idem mundus conditus et ordinatus est rationabiliter ostendit. Prius igitur de causis, deinde de ordine temporum dicamus . . . "In principio creavit Deus coelum et terram. Nihil enim aliud voluit intelligere per hoc quod dixit. In principio creavit Deus coelum et terram" et cet.' [172]. 'Quasi diceret: Primo creavit coelum et terram. Nihil enim aliud voluit intelligere per hoc quod dixit "in principio creavit" illa, nisi quod ante ea nihil creaverat Deus, et illa duo simul creasse intelligatur. Sed quid

appellet coelum et terram et quomodo secundum rationem physicorum simul creata sint demonstrare conabor.' (177).

16. For a summary of this work see E. Gilson, *History*, pp. 145–7.

17. Nicolas M. Häring, 'Thierry of Chartres and Dominicus Gundassalinus', *Medieval Studies*, XXVI (1964), p. 271.

18. Pierre Duhem, *Le Système du monde, histoire des doctrines cosmologues de Platon à Copernic*, Vol. III (Paris, 1915), pp. 184–93.

19. Dyksterhuis, p. 107.

20. *Phil.*, Lib. 2, I. '. . . divinae paginae, quae ait: *"Divisit aquas, quae sunt sub firmamento, ab his quae sunt super firmamentum"* (Gen. I). Sed, quoniam istud contra rationem est, quare sic esse non possit ostendamus, et qualiter divina Scriptura in supradictis intelligenda sit.'

21. Ibid., Lib. 1, XXXIII. 'Et hoc est, quod divina pagina dicit: *"Deum fecisse hominem de limo terrae"* (Gen. II, VII). Non enim credendum est, animam quasi spiritus, et levis, et munda, ex luto factam esse.'

22. Ibid., Lib. 1, XXXIII. '. . . quod divine pagina dicit: *Deum fecisse mulierem ex latere Adae* (Gen. II, XXI). Non enim ad letteram credendus est, constasse primum hominem. Sed dicet aliquis: eadem ratione plures homines et feminas esse creatos, et adhuc posse? Nos dicimus, verum esse, si divina voluntas esset, quia ut aliquid sit natura operante, necesse est divinam praecedere voluntatem. Item dicet hoc esse divinae potestati derogare, sic esse hominem factum dicere: quibus respondemus e contrario, id ei conferre, quia ei attribuimus, et talem rebus naturam dedisse, et sic per naturam operantem, corpus humanum creasse.

Nam in quo divinae Scripturae contrarii sumus, si quod in alla dictum esse factum, qualiter factum sit explicemus? . . . Sed quoniam ipsi nesciunt vires naturae, ut ignorantiae suae omnes socios habeant, nolunt eos aliquid inquirere, sed ut rusticos nos credere, nec rationem quaerere, ut jam impleatur propheticum: *Erit sacerdos sicut populus* (Isa. XXIV) . . . maluntque nescire, quam ab alio quaerere: et si inquirentem aliquem sciant, illum esse haereticum clamant, plus de suo caputi caputio praesumentes, quam sapientiae suae confidentes.'

23. Dyksterhuis, p. 121.

24. *Phil.*, Lib. 1, XXIII.

25. 'Sed dum moderni divini hoc audiunt, quia in Libris ita scriptum non inveniunt, obstrepunt statim, hoc ignorantes quod auctores veritatis philosophiam rerum tacuerunt, non quia contra fidem, sed quia ad aedificationem fidei, de qua laborant. non multum pertinebant; nec volunt quod aliquid supra id quod scriptum est inquiramus, set ut rusticus ita simpliciter credamus.' William of Conches, *Glossa in Boetium*, in 'Des commentaires inédits de Guillaume de Conches et de Nicholas Triveth sur La Consolation de la Philosophie de Boèce,' Charles Jourdain (ed.), *Notices et extraits des manuscrits de la Bibliothèque Imperiale*, Tome XX, 2e partie (Paris, 1862), p. 12.

26. *Phil.*, Lib. 1, XXIII. 'Nam in quo divinae scripturae contrarii sumus, si quod in illa dictum est esse factum, qualiter factum sit explicamus?'

27. *Epistulae*, XIII PL 178, col. 353A.

28. *Dialogus*, etc. (See above, fn. 2).

29. *Quaes.*, p. 66. 'Qui vero rerum ordinem tollit, insipiens est. Ab insipiente igitur hanc confusionem constitui necesse est. Minime igitur rerum ordinem tollere vel vult vel potest, quare nec hanc transpositionem stare possibile est. In philosophantis itaque animum id incidere minime conveniens est.'

30. 'Nemo itaque impie cogitet sicut quidam impii cogitaverunt nihil contra naturam scilicet contra solitum cursum nature proveniri posse.' Anon., *Liber de eodem secundus*, J.M. Parent (ed.), in *La Doctrine de la création dans l'école de Chartres* (Paris, 1938), p. 213.

31. 'De erroribus Guglielmi de Conchis' (PL 180, col. 3, 339). Lemay says, 'With

a much more comprehensive view of the universe than that of Adelard of Bath and an incomparably more systematic attempt to build up a natural philosophy on new and really rational grounds, William of Conches's *De philosophia mundi* and his other works dealing with natural philosophy come to be singled out as representing the dangerous 'novelties' dreaded by theologians and mystics. William of St. Thierry's attacks against William's works opened an important phase of the conflict of Natural Philosophy against Theology which raged during the entire course of Scholasticism in the next three or four centuries.' (*Abu-Ma'shar*, p. 194.)

32. Ibid.

33. Ibid., pp. 339, 340. 'Etiam post theologiam Petri Abaelardi, Guilelmus de Conchis novam affert philosophiam, confirmans et multiplicans quaecumque ille dixit, et impudentius addens adhuc de suo plurima, quae ille non dixit. Cuius novitatum vanitates . . .'

Elsewhere, William writes: 'Deinde creationem primi hominis philosophice, seu magis physice describens, primo dicit corpus eius non a Deo factum, sed a natura, et animam ei datam a Deo, postmodum vero ipsum corpus factum a spiritibus, quos daemones appellat . . .'

He also wrote indignantly to his friend Bernard of Clairvaux, '. . . etenim post Theologiam Petri Abaelardi, Guilelmus de Conchis novam offert Philosophiam, confirmans et multiplicans quaecunque ille dixit.'

34. Häring, 'Thierry and Dominicus', p. 277.

35. Johan Huizinga, *Men and Ideas: History, the Middle Ages, the Renaissance*, trans. by J.S. Holmes and H. Van Marle (New York, 1970), p. 190.

36. *Metalogicon*, i. 277.

37. 'Ut ait Petronius, nos magistri in scolis soli relinquemur nisi multos palpemus et insidias auribus fecerimus. Ego vero non ita . . . Sic tamen consolium meum contraxi ut vulgus profanum et farriginem scolae petulam excluderem.' Thierry of Chartres, *Commentary on Cicero's De Inventione*, fragment (MS Leyden, B.P.L. 189, F. fols. 42–7 (Leyden, 1934).

38. 'Ibi doctor cernitur ille Carnotensis cuius lingua vehemens truncat velut, ensis.' 'Metamorphosis Goliae', in Thomas Wright, *The Latin Poems Commonly Attributed to Walter Mapes*, 28, vv. 189–90 (London, 1841).

39. Häring, 'Thierry and Dominicus', p. 278.

40. *Phil.*, Lib. 4 XXXVII. 'Talis igitur quaerendus est, qui doceat: qui neque causa laudis, nec spe temporalis emolumenti, sed solo amore sapientiae doceat. Si enim propriam deligit laudem, nunquam discipulum ad suit perfectionem venire desiderat. Subtrahit ergo doctrinam, ne in eo quod plus diligit aequetur vel superetur. Si etiam spe commodi temporalis inductus, doceat, non curabit quid dicat, dum nummum extorqueat. Saepe vero plus placent nugae quam utilia. Sed si amore acientiae ad docendum acceserit, nec propter invidiam doctrinam subtrahet; nec ut aliquid extorqueat, veritatem cognitam fugiet, nec si deficiet multitudo sociorum, desinet, sed ad instructionem sui et aliorum, vigil et diligens erit.'

41. *Phil.*, Lib. 4 XXXVIII. 'Ut doceatur vero talis eligendus est qui non sit doctrinae obstrepens, nec superbus, nec videatur aliquid esse, cum nihil sit; qui magistrum ut patrem diligat, vel etiam plus quam patrem. A quo enim majora et digniora accipimus, magis diligere debemus. A patre autem rudes esse accepimus, a magistro autem sapientes, quod majus est dignius est. Plus ergo diligendi sunt boni doctores quam parentes.'

42. *Phil.*, Lib. 4 Praef. 'Superiorum voluminum series, a prima causa rerum orta, usque ad terram defluxit, pruritum aurium non continens, sed utilitati legentium deserviens, atque ideo animus stultorum non sedens. Jam enim illud ampletum est: *Erit cum sanam doctrinam non sustinebunt, sed ad sua desideria coacervabunt sibi magistros, prurientes auribus* (II Tim, IV, 3.) Quae igitur studii reliqua liberatas sperari possit, cum magistros discipulorum palpones, discipulos magistrorum judices,

legemque loquendi et tacendi impotentes cognoscumus? In paucis enim magistri, frontem, si adulantis vocem et vultum percipient; etsi sit aliquis qui magistri severitatem sequatur, ut insanus a meretricibus magister scholarum fugatur, crude-lisque vocatur et inhumanus . . .'

43. Southern, p. 31.
44. Ibid., p. 48.
45. Bernard Stambler, *Dante's Other World* (New York, 1957), p. 11.

5   The Voice of the Opposition

Science, as the twelfth-century cosmologists conceived it, was a consciously formulated, carefully worked out branch of philosophy — a distinct and separate discipline. It required the close co-operation and association of its practitioners for the purpose of pooling information and discussing hypotheses. The cosmologists envisioned an open, exciting future where the unlimited growth of scientific knowledge would bring about real progress. Such progress would yield increasing understanding of nature's operation, and this would have the twofold result of an increasingly accurate appreciation of God and of aiding mankind.

In the light of the fresh confidence felt in the rational powers of the human intellect, the cosmologists endowed the newly concretised noun *universus* and the classical concept of *natura* with singular weight and resonance. The notion of nature was put back into intellectual currency, and it became a cardinal article of faith for the new scientist that nature and the created universe operated according to basic laws and that these laws constituted a perfectly rational order, theoretically knowable by the inherently rational human mind. The intellectual confidence and the psychological sense of security which allowed such an attitude and fostered it, enhanced the dignity and value of the human species; for if nature was indeed knowable and worth understanding, then man, too, was worthy of respect, since he was capable of rationally comprehending its fundamental principles.[1]

This conviction contributed to a surge of optimism among the intellectuals at the cathedral schools — a courageous impulse towards individualist, critical and boldly creative thought. Hence the new teachers and advocates of the study of *physica*, of natural science, saw themselves as *moderni*, set apart from those who had lived in earlier times by a consciousness of possessing new knowledge and new means of continuing to gain more, and by a free, inquiring, rational intellect available for constructive use. The classic expression of this exuberant optimism is, of course, Bernard of Chartres:

We [*moderni*] are like dwarfs, supported on the shoulders of the giants [of the ancient world] and that we can see more clearly and farther than they could is due not to the acuity of our vision or the stature of our bodies, but rather to that great height of these giants, who lift us high and hold us up.[2]

This passage is freqently cited as a tribute by the twelfth-century scholars to their ancient classical literary masters; few have discerned as well, the note of confidence in the powers of the modern intellectual, the twelfth-century student of the liberal arts.

The cosmologists promoted the new science: they read the newest translations from Greek and Arabic, they taught the eager, young ambitious lay students and they argued with their more conservative colleagues. They lectured and wrote on the necessity for co-operative endeavour and for the unremitting practice of a critical examination of all existing knowledge and tradition concerning nature, to be rigorously carried on '*secundum physicam rationes*'; and they carefully discriminated between different methods and approaches to scientific inquiry. Among these, the cosmologists recognised the prime importance of an attitude of disinterested objectivity, allowing no considerations to affect scientific thinking save those clearly based on relevant data. This was, indeed, of enormous consequence for an era in which prevailed unthinking acceptance of the *auctores* (any writer of the distant past whose work or ideas were familiar). The cosmologists discussed the function of probability and inductive reasoning, and, living in the midst of evidence of technological advance, they appreciated the value of the empirical method. They saw the need for direct observation of natural phenomena and for careful measuring where this was possible. Again and again, they expressed their belief in the tremendous value of mathematical techniques for all scientific work, and they often admitted to a bias for deductive reasoning as a *sine qua non* of scientific method.

The twelfth-century scientists classified the sciences, giving due recognition to the applied sciences. They thoughtfully evaluated the education and special training required of the scientist and emphasised its importance, contrasting the properly trained intellect — able to function calmly in the uncomfortable state of doubt, of suspended judgment, or of uncertainty — with the poor performance of the untrained mind, which is apt to insist on instant certitude at whatever ultimate cost in rational proof or consistency. This period is, I believe, the first since the classical age in which the trained mind was perceived as qualitatively different from the untrained mind — the *vulgus*, the *rusticus*, as such people are scornfully termed by the new intellectual élite. Peter Abelard, for example, advised his son: 'do not believe the majority, but the better sort for the number of fools is infinite . . .'[3]

The cosmologists, in the perfect sincerity of their religious belief, groped experimentally and tentatively for new ways of accounting for the ways of God to man, at least in the matter of understanding how creation occurred. They saw difficulties and expressed them quietly, with no intention of weakening or calling into question the established tenets of their faith. In spite of the accusations and attacks made upon them, they were neither nascent heretics nor in any way connected with the dissident voices of their day. The worst we can say of them is to accuse them, as Bernard of Clairvaux did Abelard, of indulging in 'shameless curiosity'. But this shameless curiosity is the driving force of science.[4] The curiosity of the cosmologists was a quality they shared with the presocratics: secure enough to let their intellects play with the matter of experience, they engaged in free, unselfconscious speculation. Entertaining various or alternate theories and hypotheses to explain the 'bare welter of facts', the natural events in which their lives were embedded, they expressed a firm faith '. . . that through and through the nature of things is penetrable by reason.'[5] The substantial contribution made by Adelard of Bath, William of Conches and Thierry of Chartres to the inception of post-classical European science, then, is two fold: they shaped, taught, published and fought for their assumption of the basic rationality of the natural world, and they formulated and delineated in detail a succinct and essentially complete scientific methodology.

Adelard of Bath, born late in the eleventh century, taught at Paris and Laon. He travelled extensively — perhaps more than any other European writer of his day — in southern Italy, Sicily, Syria, Palestine and probably Spain. It is thought that he might have served as an officer of the Exchequer at the court of Henry I. He translated many works from Arabic on astronomy, arithmetic, chemistry and music, as well as practical treatises on such matters as the use of the astrolabe and the art of falconry. There is a story that he performed on the cither for the Queen of France. He was the first to translate Euclid's *Elements* and to introduce the use of Arabic numerals into Europe. His earlier original work *De eodem et diverso* (the title taken from a concept in the *Timaeus*) was probably written *c.* 1109, and his very popular *Quaestiones naturales, c.* 1130. Twenty copies of this document are extant, and it was frequently quoted in the subsequent centuries. In the thirteenth century, for example, Roger Bacon refers to it; and even in the fifteenth century it is quoted by such scholars as

Pico della Mirandola. Charles Homer Haskins says of him:

> Adelard occupies a position of peculiar importance in the
> intellectual history of the Middle Ages ... The first ... to
> assimilate Arabic science in the revival of the twelfth century ... he
> went out to seek knowledge for himself by travel and exploration
> ... he showed a spirit of independent inquiry and experiment quite
> his own.[6]

William of Conches was born in Normandy *c.* 1080. We know that
he taught at Paris, and it is assumed by most scholars that he was on
the faculty at the School of Chartres because John of Salisbury tells of
studying with him from 1138 to 1141. This assumption is, however,
now under attack.[7] Afterwards, perhaps when he was forced to retire
because of opposition to his scientific thought, William was employed
as tutor to Henry Plantagenet. His renown as a teacher was very
great; he is called *'opulentissimus grammaticus'* by his famous pupil,
John of Salisbury.[8] Excited by the new translations of Greek and
Arabic science beginning to appear in the West, William advocated
the study of these languages by scientists so as to be able to read the
sources, an idea not taken up again until Grosseteste and Bacon
revived it a century later. He was the first to use the noun *elementum* to
designate the basic kinds of matter in nature perceptible to the
senses.[9] His most widely-read works were his commentary on the
Timaeus, his original treatise *De philosophia mundi* and a later
revision, *Dragmaticon* (1145). Jeauneau, in his introduction to the
commentary on the *Timaeus*, says of these works:

> La *Philosophia* et le *Dragmaticon*, par le caractère synthétique,
> par leurs qualités de style et par l'élégance de leur composition,
> attirèrent tout d'abord l'attention des historiens ... leur influence
> se prolonge-t-elle de genération en genération ...[10]

Thierry of Chartres, a Breton who taught in Paris and perhaps at
Chartres, where he became chancellor in 1141, died in 1155. Little is
known about his life, and one fact — that he was the brother of
Bernard of Chartres — now appears to be fiction.[11] Some of his
students revered this brilliant and controversial master, but many
feared his 'sharp tongue that cut like a sword'. We know that his
friends had reason to trust and love him: he defended Peter Abelard at
the Council of Soissons in 1121, and he attended the trial of his

colleague, the great metaphysician Gilbert de la Porrée at Rheims in 1148, no doubt also in a friendly capacity. I have already quoted Thierry's indignant and bitter remarks on the villainous injustice of his own treatment by his hostile and fearful critics, who caused him to lose his position and reputation; they remind the reader of Abelard's *Historia calamitatum*.

Thierry's work *De sex dierum operibus* is the source of his value to the history of ideas. Raymond Klibansky has this to say of it:

> . . . his lecture on the creation of the world . . . is in fact one of the earliest attempts in Christian times to explain the formation of the world purely in terms of natural causes . . . Naïve as his account may seem . . . this first systematic attempt to withdraw cosmology from the reach of the miraculous, and to win for physical theory a relative independence from theology, gives Thierry an outstanding place among philosophers. For in the history of ideas we are concerned with those who dare to make a breach in the solid wall of prejudice which at all times dominates human thought, rather than with those who, the way once shown, follow the lead and secure the ground.[12]

That the twelfth-century cosmologists formulated a workable methodology for science fully one hundred years before the work of Robert Grosseteste, Roger Bacon and Albertus Magnus is reason enough to grant them a high place as pioneers in European science. Their work in this respect speaks for itself, and its neglect by historians can be explained only by the fascination of, and total absorption with, the effects of the impact of Aristotelian thought in the middle ages. There has been an unbroken tradition dating back to the seventeenth century that Aristotle and science were synonymous terms in the middle ages; it is time to re-examine this tradition. In the writer's opinion, it is of more significance to the history of European thought that these three men brought about the inception of a genuine intellectual revolution. This consisted of a different way of looking at nature.

Rather than the fear and hostility commonly felt towards nature in the early middle ages and the need to explain everything in terms of symbols of another reality revealed by Christian doctrine, the twelfth-century cosmologists showed a friendly and respectful attitude inviting free investigation and open appreciation of the whole cosmos. Their revolution clearly adumbrated that of the seventeenth century.

What the twelfth-century cosmologists did was to focus the new rationalist movement on a serious concentration on the natural world and a conscious inquiry into its workings. Had the temper of their time been more propitious, the world would probably not have had to wait three more centuries for a *De revolutionibus orbium*.[13] But the time was not propitious, for social and political conditions prevailed in the Western Europe of the 1150s which did not favour a climate of thought conducive to the flourishing of science. As a result, science underwent a period of retrenchment rather than of creative expansion.

The second half of the twelfth century saw the introduction into the West of Aristotle's scientific books, and of Hellenistic and Arabic works. It also produced many practical scientific texts based on observational, empirical study. Marshall Clagett points out that in the late twelfth and thirteenth centuries European scientists 'were interested in searching for principles and causes of observed things, though their approach to a theory of science was unsystematic and they were still primarily concerned with collecting the new learning and with its immediate practical applications.'[14] Typical of this kind of approach in discussions of scientific problems, were the attitudes of people like Roger of Hereford and Daniel of Morley; these Englishmen wrote a little on scientific principles, but more on practical scientific questions. Alexander Neckam had primarily a collector's interest in science, which was concentrated on practical inventions.[15] He was very interested in the utilitarian aspects of technological science and wrote amusingly of the ancient bias against this branch of learning, 'Then, the liberal arts had been the monopoly of free men, the mechanical or adulterine arts being for the ignoble.'[16] Later thirteenth-century writers on science, such as Alfred of Sarashel and Michael Scot, were more interested in describing new science and classifying it than in theory. However, Alexander of Hales did express an interest in theories of natural science. In his *Summa theologica* he discusses the problem of certitude in science and says that he believes experience to be the key. 'All human knowledge is acquired through discovery or through learning . . . All science and art happens through experience; for experience creates art.'[17]

Echoes of the cosmologists can be heard throughout the thirteenth century: Aquinas urges the necessity of studying science in the second book of the *Summa contra gentiles*;[18] Albertus Magnus writes that 'Science does not consist in simply believing what we are told, but in inquiring into the causes of natural things.'[19] Again, he says:

In science we do not have to investigate how God . . . by His free will uses that which He has created, for a miracle by means of which He manifests His power, but rather what may happen in natural things on the ground of the causes inherent in nature.[20]

Robert Grosseteste took both the rationalist and the empirical traditions developed by the twelfth-century cosmologists, and with them created a systematic account of scientific method.

From the almost pure empiricism of such practical sciences of the twelfth century as practical mathematics, atronomy and medicine, and the almost pure rationalism of the theoretical speculations . . . on scientific method, Grosseteste produced a science in which he tried to show the principles according to which the world of experience could be experimentally investigated and rationally explained.[21]

Roger Bacon lists the most troublesome impediments to the development of scientific thought, the *Offendicula:* (1) an awe of a dubious and consequently unworthy authority; (2) Clinging to established traditions; (3) Attaching value to popular prejudice; (4) The concealment of ignorance under a show of learning.[22] Dyksterhuis believes that Roger Bacon's best contribution to science was his work as sharp critic of prevailing prejudices, and thinks that he '. . . demonstrates . . . the exceptional difficulties involved in the thirteenth century in the development of science, as a result of the prevalent intellectual atmosphere.'[23] The reader of this study will see that this observation implicitly corroborates my contention that the twelfth-century scientific movement — so enthusiastically undertaken and well begun — did not, in fact, go on to fruition in the subsequent centuries on a scale that was commensurate with its brave beginnings.

There were three related but distinct factors operating in the social and political spheres in Western Europe that account for the abortion of the new scientific revolution. The first was the forming of complex political institutions — strong centralised monarchies buttressed by judicial courts and administrative departments. This new institution-making activity became increasingly purposeful and efficient in the second half of the century, especially in Germany, England, Sicily and France. More and more was the intellectual talent of the day drawn into the service of these burgeoning institutions. Evolving administrative techniques required the energies of numbers of trained personnel for the running of bureaucracies, and fresh effort had to be concentrated upon the task of revising, sifting and adding to rules and laws designed for optimum functioning of government. It became important to systematise existing laws and edicts, and this work was accompanied by ambitious undertakings involving the collecting and summarising of all kinds of available knowledge, so as to promote clarity and discrimination in its practical use by administrators.

The rapid development of the papal monarchy after the mid-eleventh century produced conditions which suggest a second reason why the work of the cosmologists was without fruitful issue in the following century. '. . . [As] the administrative system of the Church followed the general twelfth-century pattern in becoming both more complex and more subject to centralized control',[24] there was not only emphasis on systematising knowledge, but also a need for conformity in thought. With the growth in the size and functions of the papal monarchy, there grew a concomitant need for the securing and protection of its increasing power. For this reason, heresies and dissenting voices of whatever kind met with increasingly rigorous repression. We have seen how William of Conches and Thierry of Chartres were harassed and attacked on the suspicion of teaching heretical ideas; in the century after 1150, a powerful but never entirely secure papal monarchy worked unceasingly to enforce intellectual conformity.

The reception, in the thirteenth century, of the complete Aristotelian corpus, provides the third reason for the drying-up of the twelfth-century scientific revolution. Coinciding with the appearance of the universities and, soon afterward, of the new mendicant orders, this reception had a negative effect on the free development of science. Contrary to the usual opinion of historians on the impact of Aristotle's science on the growth of science in Europe, my belief is that its effect was to discourage any wide attempt to implement it.[25] In part, this was because it presented the medieval reader with so complete and convincing a theoretical picture, particularly regarding its cosmology; and also because his work proved peculiarly suitable for the business of providing a firm basis for a modern theology that could answer the needs of contemporary students of all kinds — not only theological specialists — and the needs of the Church as well. Aristotle proved useful to the religious thinkers of the period because his science and metaphysics were closely integrated and his manner of presentation allowed for many interpretations. Although the

Church began by opposing the study of Aristotle, the work was eagerly assimilated in the universities, where the study of dialectic had already been given first place in the trivium.

The so-called synthesis of Greek and Christian thought in the thirteenth century seems to have followed from Peter Abelard's *Sic et non*. His follower Peter Lombard, who assumed that this work embodied Abelard's effort to join disparate statements, ideas and points of view in Christian doctrine, wrote his own immensely influential collection, the *Sententiae*. This work presents an orderly collection of Christian doctrinal statements, pointing out discrepancies and conflicting views and suggesting solutions based on dialectic in a convincing, systematic form. The term 'reconcile' was used for this kind of treatise. (It was used seven centuries earlier by philosophers eager to end the confusions which arose when Plato and Aristotle were studied and compared.) Today historians revel in the notion of 'medieval synthesis', seeing in it a deeply satisfying resolution of all troubling dichotomies and ambiguities in both religion and experience as a whole.

But what, in fact, was this synthesis — this grand 'reconciliation'? In Gratian's great work *Concordantia discordantia canonum*, there is an admirable effort to resolve the confusion of a myriad of contradictory Church edicts and papal decrees that had accumulated for eight centuries, and to reduce this conglomeration to a workable order of canon law. I suggest that the synthesising, harmonising efforts of the century following the period of the cosmologists was, in fact, the intellectual aspect of the same tendencies in government, both papal and temporal. These efforts helped to buttress and strengthen a legitimised and stabilised institutional position.

The corporate idea was given substance by the newly evolving canon law, and from it we can infer an important use for the effort to bind, to somehow connect, disparate elements whether in philosophy or in society: all must serve, must be an integral part of a central, ordered and harmonious structure. This ideal, so brilliantly realised in the thirteenth century, helps to explain why it was that the questionings and analytical probings of tradition in all its forms, failed to win wide support among intellectually gifted men. As the twelfth century waned and the new century waxed we can trace the development of a passionate concern for tightly structured institutional forms — in law, in government, in theology, in architecture and in poetry. There was less and less room for the rebellious, rational intellect to explore, and for the open questioning which science needs.

Why did the rationalist temper of the early twelfth century give way after 1150 to scholasticism? Perhaps an explanation lies in the increasing need for certitude and intellectual support of the growing centralised institutionalism of the times. Scholastic theology — or systematic theology — satisfied a strong psychological need felt at that period to distance and objectify emotions, or, at any rate, those emotions with limited scope for open expression in the new city-oriented policy and its attendant *Weltanschauung*. A hallmark of the thirteenth-century thought is a kind of encyclopaedic didacticism, which is why the *summa* was seen as so attractive a form. For of all rationalising thought systems ever created, surely the work of Thomas Aquinas is the most consistent and most elegantly ordered. And this same impulse to create unity out of a rich complexity of experience is given supreme form in the tightly structured architectonics of Dante's *Commedia*.

The aggressive, creative drive neeed for science is replaced by an attitude of acquiescence towards the newly enhanced authority of government, both secular and ecclesiastic, and towards a Greek writer of legendary powers. Aristotle, whose extensive corpus of works were now available in Latin translation, provided a variety of attractive and plausible answers to a wide spectrum of questions both physical and metaphysical. If there is any validity in the idea that symbols of authority are emotionally central to a society's existence, then it is understandable that the best minds of the succeeding century — with a few notable exceptions — turned away from the earlier mood of open, unstructured questioning and towards the task of creating thought systems designed to augment the growing power of Church and state.

The scholastic philosophy that evolved from the purged and altered Aristotle in the second half of the thirteenth century precisely suited the Church's imperative need for security and universal acceptance. The new theology presented a tightly constructed system of thought focusing on a closed, self-sufficient, earth-centred cosmos — ideal for the conceptual framework of the Western Church. This system was coherent and related in all its parts, so that there were no loose ends, nothing unaccounted for, no inconsistencies. The genius of Thomas Aquinas fully utilised the possibilities in Aristotle's thought in creating his own vision of just such an ordered, hierarchical universe. This vision — this theology — was exactly what was needed for the authoritarian and strongly paternalistic model of a government system that was evolving at the time and reaching new heights of efficiency and power.

Such a world-view, although nominally embracing science, in effect discouraged it. For it channelled the creative energy that had previously been directed towards the rational inquiry into nature into a quite different enterprise: a highly refined and subtly rationalised philosophy in support of Western Catholic doctrine. And into this endeavour were pressed the best intellects of the time. So thoroughly was every aspect of earthly human life enmeshed in a net of ordered relationships, that the medieval mind could rest serene in a general sense of a meaningful universe. In this essentially tidy world, nature did not present a challenge to the imagination; the serenity induced by the scholastic theology was by its nature antithetical to the free thrust of the critical, inquiring intellect needed to sustain a viable scientific movement. The twelfth-century cosmologists had wished to ask new questions without envisioning any particular kind of answer; they were free to stretch their minds and imaginations in any direction that reason suggested. The scholastics wanted, in fact already possessed, a set of answers; their questions were carefully designed to produce the desired answers and to give those needed answers persuasive weight. The cosmologists had engaged in orderly ratiocination, the scholastics in systematic rationalisation. The one activity pushed outward towards the unknown, the other circled back to a safe and spiritually satisfying reality.

Finally, it seems clear that the pioneering masters of the early twelfth century whose work has been examined in this study were true scientists. Their contribution to the inception of a genuine scientific revolution stands, upon critical analysis, as substantial and valid. Had their message not been pushed aside in the course of the accelerated political change that occurred after their death, the history of European science would certainly have been different. It is just, therefore, that we revise our estimate of their proper place in medieval history and give due recognition to their achievement for science and the free use of the inquiring mind.

Notes

1.   Bernard Sylvestris was confident of man's great destiny: 'He [man] shall behold clearly principles shrouded in darkness, so that Nature shall keep nothing undisclosed.' *Cosmographia*, X, 2 (trans. W. Wetherbee, New York, 1973), p. 113.

2.   'Non esse quasi nanos, gigantium humeris incidentes, ut possimus plura eis et remotiora videre, non utique proprii visus acumine, aut eminentia corporis, sed quia in

altum subvehimur et extollimur magnitudine gigantea.' Quoted by John of Salisbury, *Metalogicon*, iii, 4. In the same vein, William of Conches writes 'Non dicit doctiores, sed perspicaciores. Non enim plura scimus quam antiqui, sed plura perspicimus. Habemus enim illorum scripta et, praeter hoc, naturale ingenium quo aliquid novi perspicimus. Sumus enim nani super humeros gigantum, ex alterius qualitate multum, ex nostra parum perspicientes.' *Glosae sur Priscien*, E. Jeauneau (ed.) in *Recherches de théologie ancienne et médiévale*, 27 (1960), pp. 212–47.

3. 'Maiori parti ne credas, sed meliori, stultorum numerus innumerabilis est, . . .' 'To Astrolabe', in *Notices et extraits*, Haureau (ed.) (Paris, 1888), p. 163.

4. Whitehead writes, '. . . curiosity means the craving of reason that the facts discriminated in experience be understood. It means the refusal to be satisfied with the bare welter of facts . . . curiosity . . . [is] the gadfly driving civilization from its ancient safeties . . .' Alfred North Whitehead, *Adventures of Ideas* (New York, 1962), p. 145.

5. Ibid., p. 112.

6. C.H. Haskins, *Studies in the History of Medieval Science* (New York, 1927), p. 42.

7. R.W. Southern, p. 71 ff.

8. *Metalogicon*, 1.5 and 2.10. It is now believed that William of Conches probably knew most of the thinkers of his day. See *Guillaume de Conches: Glosae in Juvinalem*, Bradford Wilson (ed.) (Paris, 1980), p. 83.

9. T. Silverstein, 'Elementum: Its Appearance among the Twelfth-Century Cosmologists', *Medieval Studies*, no. 16 (1954), p. 157.

10. 'Glosae super Platonem', p. 11. The *Dragmaticon* was written to correct statements originally in *Philosophiae* that had been criticised as heretical. William says, in answering his critics: 'Christianus sum, non Academicus. Cum Augustino igitur credo et sentio quotidie novas animas creari, non traduci, non ex aliqua materia, sed ex nihilo, solo iussu eas a creatore creari.' Lib. VI.

For a discussion of the different rescensions of the *Philosophia*, see Poole, *Illustrations*, Appendix VI, p. 298 following. For the influence of William of Conches, see M. Grabmann, *Handschriftlische Forschungen und Mitteilungen zum Schriftum des Wilhelm von Conches* (Munich, 1935), p. 26 following. Also see A. Vernet, 'Un Remaniement de la *Philosophia* de G. de Conches', *Scriptorium*, I (1946–7), pp. 243–59.

11. Southern, p. 70.

12. Clagett *et al.*, *Twelfth Century Europe*, p. 8.

13. Copernicus, 1543.

14. Clagett *et al.*, pp. 40, 41.

15. He also says, 'Science is acquired at great expense, by frequent vigils, by great expenditure of time, by sedulous diligence of labour, by rigorous application of mind.' *De naturis rerum*, II, 155.

16. *De naturis rerum*, II, 21.

17. *Summa*, i. tr. intro., *Quaest.* 1, c. 2. 'Omnis humana scientia est acquisita per inventionem vel doctrinam . . . Omnis scientia et ars per experientiam accidit: experientia enim fecit artem.'

18. *Summa*, II, c. 2.3. 136–7.

19. *De mineralibus*, II, Tract. 1, c. 1.

20. *De caelo et mundo*, Liber I, Tract. IV, c. 10. Albertus often reiterated his dictum: *fui et vidi expiriri*.

21. Clagett, 'Aspects of Physics', p. 43.

22. *Opus maius*, cl. 3201.

23. Dyksterhuis, *The Mechanization of the World Picture*, p. 140.

24. John P. Morrall, *Political Thought in Medieval Times* (New York, 1962), p. 43.

25. Edward Grant believes that thirteenth-century physical science was unable to

generate a scientific revolution because of the prevailing commitment to the Aristotelian system; see his *Physical Science in the Middle Ages* (New York, 1971), p. 88ff.

Bibliography

Chief Sources*

William of Conches
De philosophia mundi (PL, 90), 1127–78 (under Bede) (PL, 172, 39–102) (under Honorius Augustodunensis).
Dragmaticon, I, Rikeluis MDLXVII, G. Gratarolus (ed.) (Strasbourg, 1567).
Glosae super Platonem, Eduard Jeauneau (ed.), in *Textes philosophiques du moyen age*, XIII (Paris, 1965).
Adelard of Bath
De eodem et diverso, in 'Des Adelard von Bath Traktat', H. Willner (ed.), *Beiträge*, 4, 1. (Münster, 1903).
Quaestiones naturales, M. Muller (ed.), *Beiträge*, 31 (Münster, 1934).
Thierry of Chartres
De septem diebus et sex operibus (herein referred to as De operibus de sex dierum), *Notices et extraits*, #647, *Des Manuscrits Latins de la Bibliothèque Nationale*, Vol. 32 part 2, 167–86 (Paris, 1888).
Prologus in Eptatheucon, E. Jeauneau (ed.), in *Medieval Studies*, XVI (1954) 171–88.

Abbreviations

PL   Migne, *Patrologiae cursus completus*, Series Latins, 221 vols (Paris, 1844–64).
AHDL   *Archives d'histoire doctrinale et littéraire du moyen age* (Paris).
Beiträge   *Beiträge zur Geschichte der Philosophie des Mittelalters* (Münster).
Ueberwegs, Fried.   Ueberwegs 'Grundriss der Geschichte der Philosophie', Vol. III, *Die patrische und scholastische Philosophie*, 11 ed. B. Geyer (Berlin, 1928).
GCFI   *Gornale critico della filosofia Italiana* (Firenze).

Select Bibliography

Allbutt, T. Clifford *Science and Medieval Thought* (London, 1901)
Bäeumker, C. *Der Platonismus in Mittelalter* (Münster, 1927)
Baron, R. *Science et sagesse chez Hugues de Saint-Vincente* (Paris, 1957)
Baur, L. (ed.) 'Dominicus Gundissalinus' *De divisione philosophiae*, *Beiträge* IV (Münster, 1903)
Beaujouan, G. *L'Interdépendence entre la science scolastique et les techniques utilitaires (XIIe, XIIIe, et XIVe siècles)* (Paris, 1957)

*All translations are mine unless otherwise noted.

Beltoni, E. 'La Formazione dell'universo nel pensiero del Grossatesta' in *La Filosofia della Natura nel Medievo* (Milan, 1964)

Benson, Robert L., Constable, Giles and Lanham, Carol D. *Renaissance and Renewal in the Twelfth Century* (Cambridge, Mass., 1982)

Beth, E.W. 'Critical Epochs in the Development of the Theory of Science', *British Journal of Philos. Science*, i (1950) 27 sq.

Betzendorfer, W. *Glauben und Wissen beiden grossen Denkern des Mittelalters* (Gotha, 1931)

Bliemetzrieder, Frederich *Adelard von Bath* (Munich, 1935)

Bouard, de M. *Encyclopédies médiévales*, 'Sur la connaisance de la nature et du monde au moyen age', in *Revue de quest. hist.* (1930), pp. 258–304

Bréhier, Emile *Histoire de la philosophie: L'antiquité et le moyen age* III, trans. W. Baskin. *The Middle Ages and the Renaissance* (Chicago, 1965)

Bronowski, J. and Mazlish, B. *The Western Intellectual Tradition from Leonardo to Hegel* (New York, 1962)

Cappuyns, M. 'Bérenger de Tours', *Dictionnaire d'histoire et de géographie ecclésiastiques*, V, III (Paris, 1935)

Charma, A. 'Guillaume de Conches', *Notice biographique, littéraire et philosophique* (Paris, 1857)

Chenu, M.D. 'Naturalisme et théologie au XIIe siècle' in *Recherche de science rel.*, XXXVII (1950) pp. 5–12

—— 'L'homme et la nature. Perspectives sur la Renaissance du XIIe siècle' in *Archives d'hist. doct. et litt. du Moyen Age*, XIX (1952) pp. 39–66

—— 'Nature ou histoire?' Une controverse exégétique sur la création au XIIe siècle' in *Archives d'hist. doctr. et litt. du Moyen Age*, XX (1953), pp. 25–30

—— *La théologie au douzième siècle* (Paris, 1957)

—— *Nature, Man and Society in the Twelfth Century*, trans. J. Taylor and L. Little (Chicago, 1968)

Clagett, M. (ed.) *Critical Problems in the History of Science* (Madison, 1959)

—— 'Some General Aspects of Physics in the Middle Ages', *Isis*, XXXIX (1948)

—— Post, G. and Reynolds, R. (eds) *Twelfth Century Europe and the Foundations of Modern Society* (Madison, 1970)

Clerval, A. *Les Ecoles de Chartres, au Moyen Age* (Paris, 1895)

Courcelle, P. *Les Lettres grècques en Occident* (Paris, 1950)

Cousin, V. *Ouvrages inédits d'Abélard* (Paris, 1836)

Crombie, A.C. *Grosseteste and Experimental Science* (Oxford, 1953)

—— *Medieval and Early Modern Science*, Vol. I, rev. edn (New York, 1959)

—— (ed.) *Scientific Change* (New York, 1963)

Crombie, A.C. 'Some Attitudes to Scientific Progress, Ancient, Medieval and Early Modern', *History of Science*, 13 (1975), pp. 213–30

Curtius, Ernst Robert *European Literature and the Latin Middle Ages*, trans. W. Trask (New York, 1953)

d'Alverny, M.-Th. 'La Sagesse et ses sept filles. Recherches sur les allégories de la philosophie et des arts libéraux du IXe au XIIe siècle' *Mélanges dédiés à la memoire de Félix Grat*, I. Paris: Bibliothèque Nationale, Ms. lat. 3110, fol. 60 (1946)

Dampier-Whetham, W.C.D. *A History of Science and its Relations with Philosophy and Religion* (Cambridge, 1929)

de Ghellinck, J. *Le Mouvement théologique du XIIe siècle* (Bruges, 1948)

Delhaye, Philippe 'L'Organisation scolaire au XIIe siècle', *Traditio*, V (1947)

—— 'Un Cas de transmission indirecte d'un thème philosophique grèc', *Scholastica ratione historico-critica instouranda*, Bibliotheca Pontifici Athenaei Antonioni, (Rome, 1951)

Denifle, H. and Châtelain, A. (eds) *Chartularium univesitatis*, Vol. I (Paris, 1889) de Wulf, Maurice *History of Medieval Philosophy*, I, trans. 6th edn E.C. Messenger (London, 1952)

Dronke, P. 'New Approaches to the School of Chartres', *Anuario de estudios medievales* (Barcelona, 1969), pp. 117–40

Duhem, Pierre 'Du temps à la scholastique latin à connu de la physique d'Aristote', *Revue de philosophie* (Paris, 1909)

—— 'Thierry de Chartres et Nicolas de Cues', *Revue des sciences philosophiques et théologiques*, 3e année (1909)

—— *Le Système du monde, histoire des doctrines cosmologues de Platon à Copernic*, Vol. III (Paris, 1915)

Dyksterhuis, E.J. *The Mechanization of the World Picture* (Oxford, 1961)

Economou, George D. *The Goddess Natura in Medieval Literature* (Cambridge, Mass., 1972)

Erhardt-Siebald, von, E. and R. *The Astronomy of John Scotus Erigena* (Baltimore, 1940)

Flatten, H. *Die Philosophie des Wilhelm von Conches* (Koblenz, 1929)

Focillon, Henri *The Art of the West*, trans. J. Bony (London, 1963)

Forest, A., Van Steenberghen, E. and de Gaudillac, M. *Le Mouvement intellectuel du XIe au XIIIe siècle* (Paris, 1951)

Friedlander, Paul *Plato, an Introduction* (New York, 1958)

Garin, E. 'Contributi alla storia del platonismo medievale' in *Annali della Scuola Normale Superiore di Pisa*, XX (1951) 86 ff

—— *Studi sul platonismo medievale* (Florence, 1958)

Genicot, Léopold *Contours of the Middle Ages*, trans. L. and R. Wood (London, 1967)

Gibson, Margaret 'The Study of the *Timaeus* in the Eleventh and Twelfth Centuries', *Pensiamento*, 25 (1969), pp. 183–94

Gilson, Etienne *Reason and Revelation in the Middle Ages* (New York, 1938)

—— *History of Christian Philosophy in the Middle Ages* (New York, 1955)

Grabmann, M. *Geschichte der Scholastichen Methode*, 2 vols (Berlin, 1909–11)

—— *Mittelalterliches Geistesleben* (Munich, 1926)

—— 'Handschriftliche Forschungen und Mitteilungen zum Schriftum des Wilhelm von Conches und zu Bearbeitungen seiner naturwissenschaftlichen Werke', in *Sitzung der Bayerischen Akademie der Wissenschaften, Philos. hist. Abt.* (Munich, 1935)

Grant, Edward, 'Late Medieval Thought, Copernicus and the Scientific Revolution', in *Journal of the History of Ideas*, XXIII, no. 2 (1962), pp. 197–220

—— *Physical Science in the Middle Ages* (New York, 1971)

Green, R.H. Alan of Lille's *De Planctu Naturae*, trans. D.M. Moffat (New York, 1908)

Gregory, Tullio 'L'idea della natura nella scuola di Chartres', in *Giorn. Crit. della filos. it*, XXXI (1952), pp. 433–42

—— *Anima Mundi: La Filosofia di Guglielmo di Conches* (Florence, 1955)

—— 'Note e testi per la storia del Platonismo medievale', *Giornale critico della filosofia italiana*, XXXIV (1955)

—— *Platonismo Medievale; Studi e Ricerche* (Roma, 1958)

—— *L'idea di Natura nella Filosofia Medievale* (Florence, 1966)

—— *La Filosofia della Natura nel Medioevo: Atti del terzo congresso internazionale di filosofia medioevale, Passo della Mendola . . . 1964* (Milan, 1966)

Hadzsits, G. *Lucretius and His Influence* (London, 1935)

Häring, Nicolas M. 'The Creation and Creator of the World According to Thierry of Chartres and Clarenbaldus of Arras', *Archives d'histoire doctrinale et littéraire du moyen âge*, 22 (1955), pp. 157–64

—— 'Nine Medieval Thinkers', *Studies and Texts*, vol. I (Toronto, 1955)

────── (ed.) 'Thierry's Expositie in *Hexaemeron*', *AHDLMA*, XXII (1955)
────── *Archives d'histoire doctrinale et littéraire du moyen âge*, XXII (1955), XVII (1956), XIV (1958), XXVII (1960)
────── 'Thierry of Chartres and Dominicus Gundissalinus', *Medieval Studies*, XXVI (1964)
────── *Commentaries on Boethius by Thierry of Chartres and his School* (Toronto, 1971)
Haskins, Charles Homer 'Adelard of Bath', *English Historical Review* (London, 1911)
────── *Studies in the History of Medieval Science* (New York, 1927)
────── *Renaissance of the Twelfth Century* Meridian Books (New York, 1955)
Hauréau, B. *Singularités historiques et littéraires* (Paris, 1861)
────── *Histoire de la philosophie scolastique* (Paris, 1872)
────── 'De opere sex dierum', *Notices et extraits*, vol. XXXII, part 2 (1888)
────── *Notices et extraits de quelques mss. latins de la Bibliothèque nationale*, 6 vols (Paris, 1890–3)
Heitz, Thomas *Essai historique sur les rapports entre la philosophie et la foi de Bérenger de Tour à S. Thomas d'Aquin* (Paris, 1909)
Heule, R.J. *St. Thomas and Platonism* (New York, 1956)
Huit, C. 'Le Platonisme au moyen âge', *Annales de philosophie chrétienne*, XX (Paris, 1888)
────── 'Le Platonisme au XIIe siècle', *Annales de philosophie chrétienne*, XX (Paris, 1898)
Hunt, R.W. 'English Learning in the Late Twelfth Century', *Trans. Roy. Hist. Soc.*, 4 Ser., XIX (1936) 19 sq.
────── 'The Introduction to the 'Artes' in the Twelfth Century', *Studia mediaevalia in honorem* (Bruges, 1948)
Hyman, Arthur and Walsh, James J. *Philosophy in the Middle Ages* (New York, 1967)
Jeauneau, E. 'Prologue of the Heptateuchon', *Medieval Studies*, XVI (1954), pp. 171–5
────── 'Un représentant du platonisme au XIIe siècle: Maître Thierry de Chartres', *Memoires de la société archéologique d'Eure-et-fair*, XX (1954)
────── 'Simples notes sur la cosmologie de Thierry de Chartres', *Sophia*, XXIII (1955)
────── 'L'usage de la notion d'*integumentum* à travers les gloses de Guillaume de Conches', *Archives*, 24 (1957), pp. 35–100
────── 'Note sur l'école de Chartres', *Studi medievali*, 3e série, v. 2 (1964)
John of Salisbury *The Metalogicon*, trans. Daniel D. McGarry (Berkeley, 1955)
Jourdain, Charles 'Dissertation sur l'état de la philosophie naturelle' (Paris, 1838)
────── *Philosophie naturelle au XIIe siècle* (Paris, 1840)
Kalivoda, R. 'Zur Genesis der Naturlichen Naturphilosophie im Mittelalter', *La Filisofia della Natura nel Medievo* (Milan, 1964)
Kantorwicz, E.H. 'Plato in the Middle Ages', *Philosophical Review*, LI (1942)
Katzenellenbogen, Adolf *The Sculptural Programs of Chartres Cathedral* Norton, (New York, 1964)
Klibansky, Raymond 'Annual Reports on the Corpus Platonicus Proceedings of the British Academy', *Annual Reports* (London, 1942)
────── 'Plato's *Parmenides* in the Middle Ages and the Renaissance', *Mediaeval and Renaissance Studies* (London, 1943)
────── 'Annual Reports of the Warburg Institute' (London, 1945)
────── *The Continuity of the Platonic Tradition during the Middle Ages* (London, 1950)
────── (ed.) *Plato Latinus*, Vol. IV; *Timaeus* (London, 1962)

Langlois, Charles Victor *La Vie en France au moyen-age de la fin du XIIe au milieu du XIVe siècle*, Vol. 3, *La Connaissance de la nature et du monde* (Paris, 1928)

Lee, H.D.P. (ed.) *Timaeus*, trans. and introduction (Baltimore, 1965)

Lemay, Richard *Abu-Ma'shar and Latin Aristotelianism in the Twelfth Century* (Beirut, 1962)

Lesne, E. 'Les Ecoles de la fin du VIIIe siècle à la fin du XIIe', *Histoire de la propriété ecclésiastique en France*, V. (Lille, 1940)

Lewis, C.S. *The Discarded Image* (Cambridge, 1964)

Little, A.G. (ed.) *Roger Bacon: Essays Contributed by Various Writers on the Occasion of the Commemoration of his Birth* (Oxford, 1914)

Lloyd, G.E.R. *Reason and Experience: Studies in the Origin and Development of Greek Science* (Cambridge, 1979)

Mabilleau, L. *Histoire de a philosophie atomistique* (Paris, 1895)

Macdonald, A.J. *Berengar and the Reform of Sacramental Doctrine* (London, 1930)

MacKinney, L.C. *Bishop Fulbert and Education at the School of Chartres* (Notre Dame, 1957)

Maître, L. 'La Logique du style Gothique', *Revue Néoscolastique*, XVII (1910) 234 sq.

———— *Les Ecoles épiscopales et monastiques de l'occident depuis Charlemagne jusqu'à Philippe-Auguste* (Paris, 1924, 1965)

Mâle, Emile *L'Art religieux du XIIe siècle en France* (Paris, 1931)

Manselli, R. *Studi sulle eresie del secolo XII* (Rome, 1953)

Martin, Thomas H. *Etudes sur le Timée de Platon*, Vol. II (Paris, 1841)

Masson, H. 'Le Rationalisme de la Cathédral de Soissons', *Bulletin Monumental*, XCIV (1953), 22 sq.

McKeon, R. 'Rhetoric in the Middle Ages', *Speculum*, XVII (1942)

———— 'Aristotle's Conception of the Development and the Nature of Scientific Method', *JHI*, viii (1947), 3 sq

———— 'Medicine and Philosophy in the Eleventh and Twelfth Centuries: The Problem of the Elements', *The Thomist*, XXIV (1961)

Millor and Butler (eds) *Letter of John of Salisbury* (London, 1955)

Minio-Paluello, L. *Twelfth Century Logic: Texts and Studies*, 2 vols (Rome, 1956–68)

Monod, V. *Dieu dans l'univers*, essai sur l'action exercée sur la pensée chrétienne par les grands systèmes cosmologiques, depuis Aristote jusqu'à nos jours (Paris, 1933)

Moody, Ernest 'Empiricism and Metaphysics in Medieval Philosophy', *The Philosophical Review*, LXVII, no. 2 (1958), pp. 145–63

Morrall, John P. *Political Thought in Medieval Times* (New York, 1962)

Morris, Colin M. *The Discovery of the Individual 1050–1200* (London, 1972)

Muller, W (ed.) *'Quaestiones naturales* of Adelard of Bath', *Beiträge zur Geschichte der Philosophie*, vol. XXXI (Munich, 1934)

Murdoch, John E. and Sylla, Edith D. (eds) *The Cultural Context of Medieval Learning* (Boston, 1975)

Murray, A. Victor *Abelard and St. Bernard: A Study in Twelfth Century 'Modernism'* (New York, 1967)

Newell, John 'Rationalism at the School of Chartres', *Vivarium*, 21 (1983), pp. 121–40

Nitze, W. 'The So-called Twelfth Century Renaissance', *Speculum*, XXIII (1948)

O'Donnell, J.R. 'The Meaning of "Silva" in the Commentary on the *Timaeus* of Plato by Chalcidius', *Medieval Studies*, VII (1945)

O'Donnell, Reginald (ed.) *Chartres and Paris Revisited: Essays in Honour of Anton Charles Pegis* (Toronto, 1974)

Paetow, L.J. *The Battle of the Seven Arts* (Berkeley, 1914)

Panofsky, Irwin *Gothic Architecture and Scholasticism* (New York, 1970)

Paré, Brunet, Tremblay, *La Renaissance du XIIe siècle; les écoles et l'enseignement* (Paris, 1933)

Parent, J.M. *La Doctrine de la création dans l'école de Chartres* (Paris, 1938)

Picard-Parra, Clotilde 'Guillaume de Conches et le *Dragmaticon Philosophiae*', *Ecole nationale de Chartres* (Paris, 1943)

—— 'Une Utilisation des *Quaestiones naturales* de Sénèque au milieu du XIIe siècle', *Revue du moyen âge latin*, V (1949)

Roole, Reginald, Lane 'The Masters of the School at Paris and Chartres in John of Salisbury's Time', *English Hist. Rev.*, XXXV (1920), p. 338

—— *Illustrations of the History of Medieval Thought and Learning*, 2nd edn (London, 1932)

Pouchet, F.A. *Histoire des sciences naturelles au moyen âge* (Paris, 1853)

Raby, J.E. '*Nuda Natura* and Twelfth-Century Cosmology', *Speculum*, 43 (1968), pp. 72–7

—— *A History of Secular Latin Poetry in the Middle Ages*, 2nd edn, Vol. I (Oxford, 1967)

Renaissance and Revival in the Twelfth Century, R. Benson and G. Constable (eds) (Cambridge, Mass., 1982)

Reuter, H.F. *Geschichte der Religiosen Aufklärung in Mittelalter*, Vol. II (Berlin, 1877)

Robert, G. *Les écoles et l'enseignement de la théologie pendant la première moitié du XIIe siècle* (Paris, 1909)

Russell, J.B. *A History of Medieval Christianity* (New York, 1968)

Russell, J.C. 'Hereford and Arabic Science in England about 1175', *Isis*, XVIII (1932), 14sq.

Sanford, E. 'The Twelfth Century: Renaissance or Proto-Renaissance?', *Speculum*, XXVI (1951)

Sarton, George *Introduction to the History of Science*, Vol. II (Baltimore, 1931)

Schedler, J. 'Die Philosophie des Macrobius', *Beiträge zur Geschichte der Philosophie*, XIII, no. 1 (1916)

Schrodinger, E. *Nature and the Greeks* (Toronto, 1954)

Seznec, J. *The Survival of the Pagan Gods* (New York, 1953)

Sikes, J.G. *Peter Abelard* (Cambridge, 1932)

Silverstein, Thomas 'Daniel of Morley, English Cosmogonist and Student of Arabic Science', in *Medieval Studies*, X (1948), pp. 179–96

—— 'The Fabulous Cosmogony of Bernardus Silvestris', *Modern Philology*, XLVI (1948)

—— '*Elementum*: Its Appearance among the Twelfth-Century Cosmologists', *Medieval Studies*, XVI (1954)

—— 'Herman of Carinthia and Greek: A Problem in the New "New Science" of the Twelfth Century', in *Medievo e Rinascimento-Studi in honore di B. Nardi* (Firenze, 1955), pp. 683–99

—— 'Guillaume de Conches and the Elements', *Medieval Studies*, XXVI (1964)

Singer, C. 'Daniel Morley, an English Philosopher of the XIIth Century', *Isis*, iii (1920), p. 263 ff

Smalley, Beryl 'La Glossa ordinaria', *Recherches théologiques*, IX (1937)

—— *The Study of the Bible in the Middle Ages* (Oxford, 1952, Notre Dame, 1964)

Southern, R.W. *Medieval Humanism and Other Studies* (New York, 1970)

—— *Western Society and the Church in the Middle Ages* (Harmondsworth, 1970)

—— *Platonism, Scholastic Method and the School of Chartres*, Stenton Lecture

(Reading University Press, 1979)

Stahl, W.H. *Macrobius' Commentary on the Dream of Scipio* (New York, 1952)

Stambler, Bernard *Dante's Other World* (New York, 1957)

Steinen, W. v.d. 'Natur und Geist im zwölften Jahrhundert', *Die Welt als Geischiche*, 14 (1954), pp. 71–90

Stock, Brian *Myth and Science in the Twelfth Century, A Study of Bernard Silvester* (Princeton, 1972)

────── *The Implications of Literacy: Written Language and Models of Interpretation in the Eleventh and Twelfth Centuries* (Princeton, 1983)

Switalski, W.B. *Des Chalcidius Kommentar zu Plato's 'Timaeus'* (Münster, 1902)

Taton, R. *Reason and Chance in Scientific Discovery*, trans. A. Pomeraur (New York, 1962)

Thorndike, Lynn *Magic and Experimental Science*, Vol. 2 (New York, 1923)

────── 'More Manuscripts of the *Dragmaticon Philosophia* of William of Conches', *Speculum*, XX (1945)

────── *The Relation Between Byzantine and Western Science and Pseudo-Science Before 1350* (Janus, 1964)

Ueberweg, F. 'Le Rationalisme de J. Scot', *Revue scolaire philosophique et théologique* (1907)

────── *Grundriss der Geschichte der Philosophie*, Parts I and II, B. Geyer (ed.) (Berlin, 1928)

Van Winden, J.C.M. *Chalcidius on Matter, His Doctrine and Sources: A Chapter in the History of Platonism* (Leyden, 1959)

Vernet, A. 'Un Remaniement de la *Philosophia* de Guillaume de Conches', *Scriptorium*, I (1946–7)

────── 'Une Epitaphe inédite de Thierry de Chartres', *Recueil de travaux offert à C. Brunel*, ii, (Paris, 1948), pp. 660–70

Vyver, A. van der 'Les Etapes du developement philosophique du haut moyen âge', *Rev. belge philol. hist.*, viii (1929) 425sq.

────── 'L'Evolution scientifique du haut moyen âge', *Archeion*, XIX (1937)

Webb, C. *John of Salisbury* (London, 1932)

Wedel, Thomas O. *The Medieval Attitude toward Astrology particularly in England* (Oxford, 1920)

Weinberger, Julius *A Short History of Medieval Philosophy* (Princeton, 1964)

Weisheipl, James A. 'Classification of the Sciences in Medieval Thought', *Mediaeval Studies*, 27 (1965), pp. 54–90

Werner, K. 'Die Kosmologie und Naturlehre des scholastischen Mittelalters mit spezielles Beziehung auf Wilhelm von Conches', *Sitzungsberichte der Akademie der Wissenschaften zu Wien*, LXXV (1873)

Wetherbee, Winthrop *Platonism and Poetry in the Twelfth Century* (Princeton, 1972)

White, Lynn, Jr 'Natural Science and Naturalistic Art in the Middle Ages', *History*, LII (1947)

────── 'Science and the Sense of Self: The Medieval Background of a Modern Confrontation', *Daedalus*, 107, 2 (1978), pp. 47–59

Willner, H. (ed.) *'De eodem et diverso' of Adelard of Bath* (Munich, 1906)

Wolff, Philippe *The Awakening of Europe*, I (Baltimore, 1968)

Wright, Thomas *The Latin Poems Commonly Attributed to Walter Mapes* (London, 1841)

────── (ed.) *'De naturis rerum' of Alexander Neckam*. Rolls Series, vol. XXXIV (London, 1863)

Wrobel, Z. (ed.) Platones *'Timaeus'* interprete Chalcidio (Leipzig, 1876)

Name Index

Absolam of St Victor 87
Adelard of Bath 15, 17, 23,
   40–2, 53–80 *passim*, 98,
   99
Alan of Lille 80
Albertus Magnus 100–2
Alexander of Hales 101
Alexander Neckam 101
Alfred of Sarashel 101
Anselm of Aosta 38, 39, 45,
   81
Aquinas 101, 105
Aristotle 11–25 *passim*, 37,
   43, 62, 71, 100–5 *passim*
Augustine 9–13 *passim* 65,
   85

Berengar of Tours 11, 24, 38,
   39
Bernard of Chartres 36, 91,
   96, 99
Bernard of Clairvaux 98
Bernard Silvestris 19, 44, 54
Boethius 10, 15, 38, 62, 63

Chalcidius 12, 15, 68
Constantinus Africanus 65

Daniel of Morely 101
Dante 20, 91, 105

Fulbert of Chartres 66

Galen 65, 68
Garnerius of Rochefort 57
Gerbert of Aurillac 62, 65

Gilbert de la Porrée 100
Gratian 104
Gundisalvo 58, 59

Hermes Trismagistus 37
Honorius of Autun 41, 43,
   55, 84, 88
Hugh of St Victor 15, 18–21
   passim, 39, 41, 58, 67

Isidore of Seville 10

John of Salisbury 17, 36, 44,
   70, 88
John Scotus Erigena 37

Lanfranc 38

Manegold of Lautenbach 51
Martianus Capella 10, 44
Michael Scot 101

Pedro Alfonso 50, 51
Peter Abelard 15, 19, 25, 63,
   65, 72, 78, 82, 86–8,
   97–9, 104
Peter Lombard 104
Plato 9, 13–28 *passim*, 36,
   63–72 *passim*, 104
Plotinus 9, 13

Rabanus Maurus 38
Richard of St Victor 55
Robert Grosseteste 16, 66,
   71, 99–102 *passim*
Robert of Melun 17